Responsibility for the Generation

Responsibility for the Generation

Atef Meshreky

Responsibility for the Generation

Written by Atef Meshreky
Revised and edited by Sarah Park & J. Y. Hong
Designed by Jane Park
Published by Jungmi Kim

Copyright 2014 ⓒ Anchor Publishing & Media
469-171 Sooyoudong, Kangbookgu, Seoul, Korea
Tel : 010-4804-0806, 070-8253-9301
E-mail : anchorpnm@gmail.com

ISBN 978-89-967297-2-3   03230

Scripture taken from the New King James Version.
Copyright ⓒ 1982 by Thomas Nelson, Inc.
Used by permission. All rights reserved.

*The Christian life is a life
of fellowship and responsibility.*

INTRODUCTION ········ 8

PART I
BIBLICAL PRINCIPLES CONCERNING OUR
RESPONSIBILITY TOWARD THE GENERATION ········ 13
1. Understanding the mind of God concerning blessings ···· 18
2. Understanding the difference between special
   blessings and general blessings ········ 33
3. Discerning the time in which we live ········ 41

PART II
HOW CAN WE BE RESPONSIBLE FOR THE GENERATION? ···· 59
4. Understanding the main features and characteristics
   of the generation ········ 63
5. Features and weaknesses of our generation ········ 71
6. Remedies to help with the weaknesses of our
   generation ········ 76

Table of CONTENTS

PART III
HOW CAN WE BLESS OUR GENERATION? ···· 87
7. Searching the Scriptures to understand God's mind concerning the blessing of the generation ···· 89
8. A generation of the end times ···· 99

PART IV
RECEIVING A NEW FILLING AND ANOINTING OF THE HOLY SPIRIT ···· 115
9. Principles in receiving a new filling of the Holy Spirit ···· 121

PART V
UNDERSTANDING THE COVENANT RELATIONSHIP ···· 139
10. Characteristics of the covenants ···· 151
11. The new covenant ···· 174
12. Experience the fruits and blessings of the covenant ···· 183

INTRODUCTION

I had never thought that I would be set apart for the Lord in full time ministry.

All my dreams and ambitions were focused on medicine, which I studied and was passionate about. However, one day during my medical studies, the Lord drew near me in a very special way and called me to serve Him. The burning coal of love that the Lord has put in my heart on that day and at that time was sufficient to change all my dreams and desires toward the Lord and to serving Him. Therefore, as soon as I completed my medical school I joined this divine calling in the Coptic Church in Egypt to be a celibate brother consecrated and set apart for ministry. This was in 1970.

After a few years, I had a great longing for a life of holiness. I used to compare my spiritual reality to the picture of the true Christian life portrayed in the New Testament. By so doing, I realized the extent of my poverty, helplessness and stumbling.

I sought the counsel of the spiritual leaders of my generation and I searched for a practical outlet to what I truly desired and longed for. Finally, the Lord led me into years of seclusion to worship, study the word of God and understand His will. I went to one of the monasteries in the south of Egypt where I remained in seclusion for several years fasting, praying, studying the word of God and waiting upon the Lord. He visited me with His grace through very special closeness and He revealed to me rich mysteries. As a result, my feet were guided unto the way of the deep life in the Spirit.

When I went back to my ministry I longed again for another time of seclusion. In this other seclusion, I spent most of the time going deep in the word of God and studying the books of the Scriptures from Genesis to Revelation.

After that, I moved from the South of Egypt to the capital, Cairo, where I spent four years in spiritual seclusion during which the Lord led me to discover the wells of the early fathers of the Church. These wells overflowed upon me, a deep and fulfilling worship in the Spirit, from its rich springs and sources. As I was quenched by this living water of the Church of God in its early apostolic and patristic ages, I felt a great responsibility to share and commit what I received from the Lord to the body of Christ, as much as I can.

The purpose of this is: to deepen the spiritual life enabling the Church to face the challenges of the end times; to reunite the mind of Christ in the Church east and west because these wells reflect the mind of the Church before the division; and to prepare the bride for the second coming of Christ and for the wedding of the Lamb!

This book presents to believers and ministers some necessary guidelines and spiritual principles that enable them to realize their responsibility toward this generation and how to bless it and minister to it. The Christian life is a life of fellowship and responsibility(Romans 1:5).

Our generation has specific features, being so much influenced by the media, which has massively evolved and became governed by factors that are different from previous generations. It is also 'a generation of conflicts and struggles'; a generation that exists at a time of global conflicts everywhere and in every field, in the midst of which the generation aspires for self-fulfillment. First and foremost, we should not forget that it is the generation of the end times.

The challenges are numerous; yet, *where sin abounded, grace abounded much more* (Romans 5:20).

Dr. Atef Meshreky (Fr. Seraphim)
Shine International

I

BIBLICAL PRINCIPLES CONCERNING OUR RESPONSIBILITY TOWARD THE GENERATION

How do we begin to understand our responsibility toward this generation? It is easy to cover this topic in a broad and general way, and we usually like to bring many thoughts and ideas from different sources to talk about how to be responsible for the generation. However, if we truly desire to be responsible for this generation, we must accept a commission from God. We cannot be a channel of blessing for this generation without receiving a real commission from God.

How can we receive such a commission? You may quickly answer by saying that we can pray for it, ask God to give us His commission, and to make us a channel of blessing. And because God is loving and merciful, He will surely answer us. However, let us think for a moment about the fact that there are ministers of God who have very deep blessings, and able to bless powerfully, while others only bless in a general and superficial way. What is the reason for this difference? When God sees a man or a woman who is well prepared for an important task, He sends His commission and blessing. However, if we are not properly prepared, we cannot be His channel of blessing and thus unable to minister or bless powerfully.

Then how can we be prepared in a proper way? There is only one way. It is to go deeper into the word of God and in our relationship with Him.

Being responsible for the generation may mean many things. However, it is important to: understand the mind of God on this topic; understand what the responsibility for the generation really means; understand how we can be in an intimate relationship with God for that special purpose; and understand what the real need is, in the time in which we now live.

Unfortunately, this generation has not been trained to be disciples of the Bible. We have been trained to simply listen to an uplifting sermon and enjoy a time of worship, and then return back to our lives. Paul, however, spoke about the different types of nourishment for the inner man: milk and meat. There is a place for milk. Milk is lovely, sweet and easily digestible, but it is only a food for children. Meat is not sweet and difficult to digest, but it is so needed to mature a person into full maturity. It is a food needed for spiritual maturity. In this way, we now need to go through some meat and accept the difficulty of its digestion, but in this way we can grow and become spiritually mature.

> John 20:21 *So Jesus said to them again, "Peace to you! As the Father has sent Me, I also send you."*

Notice that these were the first words that came from the mouth of the Lord after the resurrection. So these words must be the most important message for His disciples. *As the Father has sent Me, I also send you.* According to this, a true believer is a sent person, or a missionary. We, as believers, are called to be missionaries. There is a place for special callings, such as when a person is called to be a missionary for a particular country. But there is also a general calling for every believer, to be a missionary in the proper sense of the word. Jesus called us to be missionaries, and speaks of this calling right after His resurrection.

Why did Jesus use these particular words as His first

words after the resurrection to address His disciples? It was because, after the resurrection, Jesus had completed a spiritual process, which usually originates in a person's heart. Jesus changes the heart, and He actually grants a person a bigger heart. In the Hebrew language of the Old Testament, the words *heart* and *spirit* are the same.

After the fall of man, the spirit, which is the heart, collapsed. Man became self-centered. He began to think only of himself, concerned only with his own needs, and ignoring the needs of others around him. Man was even ready to fight in order to take care of his own needs at the expense of others. This is the main disease and ailment that affected humanity after the fall.

However, Jesus took this sickness away from man when He died and was raised again. Salvation means giving a person a new heart that is no longer collapsed and self-centered. Instead, it is transformed into a heart that is ready to go out and to think of others. In this sense, every true man of God is called to be a missionary.

So now the question that needs to be answered is: what are we called to do and what is our responsibility toward this generation? We need to be disciples of the Bible and find our answer in Scripture.

ONE
Understanding the mind of God concerning blessings

> Genesis 12:1-2 *¹Now the Lord had said to Abram: "Get out of your country, from your family and from your father's house, to a land that I will show you. ²I will make you a great nation; I will bless you and make your name great; and you shall be a blessing."*

We can see in this passage that the first important principal is: a man of God must first be blessed and only then, can he bless others. If we are truly concerned with our generation, we must take our place in the spirit as a person who is blessed, and who is able to bless others.

This will lead us to understand the mind of God concerning the meaning of the word *blessing*. Although we have read the word *blessing* many times throughout the Bible, we may have never really thought about the mind of God regarding this word and its true biblical meaning. Let us go through some thoughts in the Bible regarding the meaning of the word *blessing* and the mind of God concerning this word. This will give us a deeper understanding about how we can become blessed and how we can bless others.

Essentially, God's purpose was that man would be a channel of blessing. God is the source of every blessing because of His infinite goodness and emphatic desire to bless man who is the crown of creation. It is a simple yet profound truth, that when man receives blessing from God, he is able to release the blessing to others. We are not the source of the blessing, and we cannot receive the blessing just to keep the blessing for ourselves. We must release the blessing to others. This means that if we really want to bless the generation, we must be that channel between God and the people.

In response to this, you may say that you already understand that we are a channel between God and His people. Then, I would like to ask a question. When you pray or speak with God, are you able to receive blessings each and every time you communicate with Him? You might answer, "Of course, it happens all the time," without differentiating between receiving a blessing for your own life, and a real blessing for the generation.

You may even use incorrect terms in your conversation, and say, "I am really blessed because God has provided everything I need." Yes, this is a real blessing. However, the Bible clearly says that this type of blessing is not only available to His children, but also available to the unbeliever and even the wicked.

> Matthew 5:45 *that you may be sons of your Father in heaven; for He makes His sun rise on the evil and on the good, and sends rain on the just and on the unjust.*

For example, material things are a blessing available for everybody. One might even say, "I had a lot to do today and had to go to many places, and God helped me and enabled me to do everything. It was a blessed day!" And yes, it was a blessed day.

But this type of blessing is also available to the unbeliever, because God is merciful and He is good. The Bible speaks of God as a provider who provides for everybody, even for the wicked and those who do not believe in Him. The wicked and the unbeliever also eat, dress, live, and are provided for because God is merciful. But God has in his stores, a very different type of blessing. It is kept for those who want to really bless others in a special way: those who do not live for themselves, who are not self-centered, but are thinking of others in the way that God thinks of others.

When God created Adam, He blessed him and gave him dominion over all creation, so that he would be a blessing to all the other creatures.

> Genesis 1:28 *Then God blessed them, and God said to them, "Be fruitful and multiply; fill the earth and subdue it; have dominion over the fish of the sea, over the birds of the air, and over every living thing that moves on the earth."*

After the fall, the channel, through which God's blessing could extend through all of creation, was no more. Then came the flood, after which God spoke to Noah and extended the same words of blessing as was given to Adam.

> Genesis 9:1 *So God blessed Noah and his sons, and said to them: "Be fruitful and multiply, and fill the earth."*

However, corruption increased yet again through Noah's descendants and God was greatly grieved. They could no longer be a channel of blessing and God sought to restore that channel once more. God found Abraham and blessed him in the same manner. After Abraham, came Moses and the law. God set apart the tribe of Levi, and gave to them a special commission. The core of this commission was to bless His people. God even gave them the main words that could be used in blessing the people. We can find these words in the book of Numbers.

> Numbers 6:22-26 *[22] And the Lord spoke to Moses, saying: [23] "Speak to Aaron and his sons, saying, 'This is the way you shall bless the children of Israel. Say to them: [24] "The Lord bless you and keep you; [25] the Lord make His face shine upon you, and be gracious to you; [26] the Lord lift up His countenance upon you, and give you peace."'*

We can see an interesting point here in these verses. According to the scholars, God's name 'Jehovah' is mentioned three times in reference to the blessing in this passage. This signifies that even in the Old Testament the blessing comes from the Father, the Son, and the Holy Spirit. It is clear that the blessing is a very important item in the mind of God, and because of this, the three persons of the trinity share in the releasing of the blessing to mankind. This also means that the blessing is differentiated and has many aspects. Let us read the above passage again, looking at the distinct differences between how the Father, the Son, and the Holy Spirit, bless the people.

The blessing of the Father reads, *Bless you and keep you.* The Hebrew language here is interesting. 'Keep you' means that a hedge is kept around the person. We read in the book of Job that Satan came to criticize and accuse Job. Satan said to the Lord, *You have put a hedge around him* (Job 1:10). We have to pause here and understand the difference between general blessings and special spiritual blessings. Special blessing means that there is a hedge around a person and Satan is unable to reach him easily. This hedge is not available as a general blessing. This hedge is put in place because when a person is commissioned to bless others he comes into direct conflict with the enemy. Although the enemy attempts to hinder him and attack him, he is unable to do so because of the hedge.

The blessing of the Son reads, *His face shine upon you. Shine* in the Hebrew language is also significant. It means light, radiance, and warmth. Sin caused darkness but salvation restored us to the real blessing of God. Let us think about what it means to be radiant by the blessing of the Son. Do you know what it means to be truly radiant? It means that when you go out onto the street, people will notice you and ask, "what is the source of your life, why are you so different?"

When I was a young brother, I recall meeting a dear friend who was a missionary in charge of a worldwide ministry. When he came to visit my country, he was in his 60's. I was invited to attend a meeting that he was leading. When I saw him I was greatly impacted and impressed because he was so radiant, and even appearing to be young, as if he was in his 30's. He was full of love, light, and life.

During the day he led a pastor's conference and he spoke of an experience from his home in America. There was a supermarket close by which he frequented, and one day the supermarket owner ran after him as he was leaving. My friend was surprised and asked the owner if there was a problem.

The owner answered, "No, I just wanted to ask you a question. Are you by any chance searching for a job?"

My friend was again surprised and responded, "No, I don't need a job, but why are you asking me about a job?"

The owner was persistent and continued to press a job upon him, offering him free groceries, even offering him a very high salary. My friend politely declined saying that he had his own responsibilities to take care of, but asked the reason for such a request. Finally, the owner explained the real reason for his persistence, "I would like for you to work here because whenever you come into my store for groceries I notice that every person in the store stops doing what they are doing to observe you, and to be around you, although you are oblivious of this obvious gathering. I see people walking into the store just to glance at you and then leave without buying anything. So I thought that if you came to work for me, my supermarket would always be full."

This is a true story that happened about 50 years ago, but I have read many similar stories of saints who lived in the 4th century who also had such radiance. When we hear accounts of such radiance we feel ashamed because we are not radiant in the same manner. However, we must remember that the grace of salvation we have already received has the power of radiation. Unfortunately, it is imprisoned within us.

When Paul said we must work out our salvation, he also said that we must do it with trembling and fear. We must be completely serious as we work out our salvation because there are many treasures in the grace of salvation. When the treasures are released, then we will be truly radiant, making a real impression on others around us. We will be stopped on the streets and people will inquire, "What is the source of your life?"

And then we will be able to confidently and powerfully speak the name of Jesus Christ. Much effort is being made in order to reach the nations and to spread the Gospel. Unfortunately, people often do not really accept the message of Jesus and the Gospel. The reason for this is because we are not truly radiant.

The blessing of the Holy Spirit reads, *Lift up His countenance upon you and give you peace.* This means that He deals with the results of sin. Sin causes our heads to be cast down, because we know in our hearts that we grieve God with our many sins and we are sometimes imprisoned in chronic sin. We know that we are not living a victorious Christian life. Because of this, it is as if our inner head is cast down. The Holy Spirit comes to lift up our heads. In the Hebrew language, it means giving honor, shield, peace, and security.

There is a very important point in the beginning of Numbers chapter 6. The chapter begins by speaking about the Nazirite. We must also note that the chapter ends with a blessing. This means that according to God's mind, we cannot release the fullness of God's blessing to others unless we are Nazirites. In the Old Testament, a Nazirite was someone who gave himself to God and His service, for a set period of time. The Nazirite abandoned everything, gave himself totally to God, and took important precautions. It was a very serious life, abstaining from the pleasures of the world, even to the point of leaving family relationships, not even released to share in the death of a family member.

God is still searching for the one who desires to live seriously with Him. The Christian life is a sacrificial life and it may not be an easy one, but it is a life of purpose that comes with the help of grace. We often forget about our place in the heavens, and because of this we see our sacrifices here on earth as being huge sacrifices. We must remind ourselves that we do not belong to this world. God has raised us and seated us in the heavenly places. We are not 'here' in the world, but must be 'there' in the heavenly places. We are here as visitors, strangers, here for a purpose, and when it is finished we will return to our home. When someone goes to a place for a purpose, he is ready to sacrifice everything to fulfill his purpose. When we have this mindset, the sacrifices of this life are not difficult because it is a simply a small moment in time and we maintain a single focus for our purpose. We are not distracted with other things because we would like to finish everything and go back home.

I am here as a visitor from Egypt. After a week I will return home. And so, I am only interested in my role and purpose while I am here because I do not belong here. I have nothing to distract me here. It is easy for me to do this because I know that I am here temporarily for a purpose. Back in my own country, it is more difficult because it seems that I belong there and I can become easily distracted. Therefore, we must constantly remind ourselves everyday that we do not belong here, and that we belong to heaven; only here temporarily for a purpose.

God looks at the heart, and when he sees a person living in this manner, He will entrust the blessing of others to that person. In the time of Moses, the Nazirites were only a few in number, and they were Nazirites for only a certain period of time. However, in the New Testament, we as Christians are also Nazirites set apart for Him; all the time and all throughout our lives. We must ask ourselves whether we are truly living as Nazirites.

Let us look at some verses in the Bible to see how God blesses us in the New Testament and how we should bless others.

> Ephesians 1:3 *Blessed be the God and Father of our Lord Jesus Christ, who has blessed us with every spiritual blessing in the heavenly places in Christ.*

God has already released every spiritual blessing. Everything is released to us, but the question is, whether we are actually able to receive everything. I think we know this verse in Ephesians very well but we merely read it and do not fully grasp what it means for us.

There is a mystery in this verse; God said that He released to us every spiritual blessing but no one can say that he has received every possible blessing from Him. This actually depends on the condition of our heart and spirit. Practically speaking, we must be truly concerned with the spiritual state of our hearts, and keen to grow more in spirit. And whenever our hearts grow more, we receive revelation and inspiration, and we are able to discover more of the blessings that have been released by God, which could not be discerned within us before. It is as though seeds have been planted into our hearts when we were saved, but can now be opened up to understand new blessings and to release those blessings.

There are other seeds deep down in our hearts, which are not growing. If our spirits and hearts do not grow, they will only remain as seeds. Unfortunately, blessings can remain trapped deep within our hearts until the point of our death. And when we go before the throne of God at the end of our lives, He will say to us, "Did you know? You have only received a small portion of my blessings, and others are still imprisoned within your heart. There are a lot of seeds still in your heart, and this grieves me."

I recall a story of a pastor, who lived about 40 years ago in America. He received a true vision from God. God told him to teach the people that when many end their earthly lives and come to Him, most of them have only received one fourth of what was prepared for them. Unfortunately, we are easily self-satisfied. We must stir our spiritual hunger all the time. When our spiritual hunger stops, our hearts become limited, unable to receive blessings and unable to release the blessing to others.

> 1 Peter 3:9 *not returning evil for evil or reviling for reviling, but on the contrary blessing, knowing that you were called to this, that you may inherit a blessing.*

> Romans 12:14 *Bless those who persecute you; bless and do not curse.*

There are two main points in these verses. Peter tells us that we cannot receive more of our inheritance until we bless others. He tells us to bless so that we may inherit a blessing. He is saying that if we are unable to release, then we cannot receive. We must remember that our human nature is very weak, and we are easily self-satisfied with the blessings we have. I think every one is living within a portion of his blessings, content and thankful for those blessings. However, we do not realize that blessings are a stream passing through us and we are only channels.

When it is stagnant it is no longer a blessing, no longer shining, and can no longer impact others around us. The stream must be running and flow as a living stream that can embrace and bless others. You must ask yourselves: what is the state of my inner stream? Is it stagnant, or is it a flowing stream of blessing?

If you are not receiving new blessings, it means that the stream is stagnant. Remember that new blessings are not material blessings; it is not something you need to own for yourself, but a precious thing that is revealed to you by God, who opens His heart, and then you will receive this like a jewel; a treasure. You will then keep it in your heart and meditate on it and then you can truly receive it to bless others in a special and powerful way.

Paul, in Romans 12:14, is challenging us to bless, even in the midst of persecution and curse. He tells us to bless those who persecute us. When we receive persecution, oppression, and bad things from others, we find that our hearts are changed - to become angry, sad, and tense and in turn, causing the blessings to stop. The question is, when we are challenged, can we still maintain a peaceful heart? When anger comes into our hearts, the flow of blessing stops. When bad lusts come into our hearts, the blessing stops. When strife with others comes into our hearts, the blessing stops. We must keep our hearts peaceful and transparent so that the stream of blessing flows freely and abundantly.

TWO
Understanding the difference between special blessings and general blessings

The main purpose of God is to bless people, and He is always seeking a channel for that blessing. There are general blessings of God that reach every person because God is good and merciful, but there are also special blessings coming out from the redemptive work of Christ from the cross.

General blessings flow from God the Father, out of His goodness and mercy, but there is a special blessing that flows from the Son, out of His redemptive work on the cross. General blessings can reach any person, whether he is a believer or an unbeliever. This depends on the goodness of the Father. But the special blessing, coming from the redemptive work of Christ, has the purpose of changing a person to find Christ as the Savior. The general blessings are mainly focused on the material life that we live here on earth. But the special blessings, coming from the redemptive work, are mainly focused on our eternal and spiritual life.

General blessings speak to the people through the earthly and material life, so that they can find God's mercy. But special blessings speak to people concerning their eternity, their eternal fate. This type of blessing is mainly focused to awaken the heart and the spirit of the person so that they may understand their eternal fate. Paul wrote in Ephesians 1:3, that God the Father has blessed us with all the blessings in Jesus Christ.

It is clear that Paul, being a Jew, knew that God the Father blessed the people from the Old Testament according to their earthly life. Paul knew that in the Old Testament, people understood blessings as being related to their finances, land and possessions. Now Paul wanted to remind the Church that there was another type of special blessing, which was locked in the stores of God. However, after the redemptive work was completed on the cross, this special type of blessing could now be unlocked to flow and be released. Before the redemptive work of Christ, people were unable to understand this type of blessing of heavenly treasures because these were related to the mysteries of the heavenly realm.

Paul, in his letter to the Ephesians, writes that we, as Christians, have been seated in the heavenly places. So we are no longer of the earth, focusing on earthly things. Earth is no longer our land and home. We do not belong here and we have nothing to take from here. We have been seated in the heavenly places and we are actually going into a new realm. And we only need to discover what is in the new realm. Paul tells us that there are many treasures waiting there, and they have been unlocked and we can now begin to receive them. He also tells us to take care not to speak anymore about things related to earth.

It is very important for us to understand the difference between the two types of blessings in the Bible. If we are still waiting for God to bless us in our finances and in our possessions, then we are putting ourselves in the Old Testament; we are no longer Christians of the New Testament, but are Jews of the Old Testament. There are two different plans, or economies, in the Bible: the Old Testament and the New Testament. The economy of the Old Testament is an earthly one, while the economy of the New Testament is a heavenly one. The people of the Old Testament were unable to understand anything related to the heavens, because after the fall of man, darkness came upon human beings. But because God is merciful, He came down to speak to the people in their environment; in their realm. God began to train the people, beginning in the earthly realm, and lead them into the time of Christ, so that they would be able to receive the Holy Spirit, push out the darkness, bring light, and be able to understand the heavenly things. And because of this, the wars of the people living in Israel of the Old Testament were earthly wars. Now our battles are heavenly battles with an unseen enemy. Israel's blessings were earthly blessings of a promised land in Judea, but our blessings are in the heavenly realm.

So if we are still waiting for earthly blessings, we are looking to God through the darkness of the fall, and we have not lifted up the veil that came from darkness.

> 2 Corinthians 3:12-18 *[12] Therefore, since we have such hope, we use great boldness of speech - [13] unlike Moses, who put a veil over his face so that the children of Israel could not look steadily at the end of what was passing away. [14] But their minds were blinded. For until this day the same veil remains unlifted in the reading of the Old Testament, because the veil is taken away in Christ. [15] But even to this day, when Moses is read, a veil lies on their heart. [16] Nevertheless when one turns to the Lord, the veil is taken away. [17] Now the Lord is the Spirit; and where the Spirit of*

the Lord is, there is liberty. ¹⁸ But we all, with unveiled face, beholding as in a mirror the glory of the Lord, are being transformed into the same image from glory to glory, just as by the Spirit of the Lord.

In this passage, Paul speaks about the veil that came upon the mind. This veil occurred at the time of the fall, and it was there on the minds of all the people at that time. Because of that veil people began to worship idols. Even Israel, who received the law and saw God on the mountain as fire, who had many prophets speaking to them on behalf of God, went back to worshiping idols many times. This was because of that veil.

Paul says that if we live in the power of the Spirit, that veil is torn out, and we will be able to see the glory of God with the inner sight of the heart. This is one of the treasures and blessings of the New Testament. Unfortunately, our minds are still so focused on earthly blessings.

As people of the New Testament we must have a deep hunger in our spirits toward the heavenly blessings. The real believers of the early centuries almost completely ignored all the earthly things and they were even happy be poor because they focused on the heavenly things.

1 Corinthians 1:26-30 *²⁶ For you see your calling, brethren,*

> *that not many wise according to the flesh, not many mighty, not many noble, are called. ^{27} But God has chosen the foolish things of the world to put to shame the wise, and God has chosen the weak things of the world to put to shame the things which are mighty; ^{28} and the base things of the world and the things which are despised God has chosen, and the things which are not, to bring to nothing the things that are, ^{29} that no flesh should glory in His presence. ^{30} But of Him you are in Christ Jesus, who became for us wisdom from God - and righteousness and sanctification and redemption.*

From these verses we can see that God is pleased with the poor because they are not bound to earthly things. As such, He can easily draw them to salvation through Christ, and their eyes can easily open up to see the heavenly things.

Remember, Paul came from a wealthy family. And upon following Christ he lost everything, including, dignity, honor, and wealth; but considered all of these losses to be large winnings.

> Philippians 3:7-10 ^{7} *But what things were gain to me, these I have counted loss for Christ. ^{8} Yet indeed I also count all things loss for the excellence of the knowledge of Christ*

Jesus my Lord, for whom I have suffered the loss of all things, and count them as rubbish, that I may gain Christ [9] *and be found in Him, not having my own righteousness, which is from the law, but that which is through faith in Christ, the righteousness which is from God by faith;* [10] *that I may know Him and the power of His resurrection, and the fellowship of His sufferings, being conformed to His death.*

Paul considered his losses as his gain, and he began to teach the Churches the art of being content with Christ. Be mindful however, Paul was not teaching poverty, but how to be rich in Christ, also reminding them that there is always a cost. It is not wrong to possess money or wealth, but you must know that wealth is not something that you can possess. If you possess money, then money will possess you. If you think that money is your possession, then money will enslave you.

The Bible teaches us that if you have money you are a steward because money belongs to God and He has placed you as a steward over the money. Therefore, we must be faithful stewards, and learn the art of stewardship through the Holy Spirit. Furthermore, we must accept that we are strangers in this land and learn to be content.

1 Timothy 6:6-8 *⁶ Now godliness with contentment is great gain. ⁷ For we brought nothing into this world, and it is certain we can carry nothing out. ⁸ And having food and clothing, with these we shall be content.*

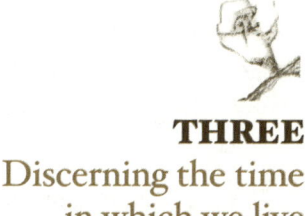

THREE
Discerning the time in which we live

When you are visiting a country and have a task set before you, it is usually understood that only a limited amount of time is available for that task. When a person is sent for a task, he usually asks about the time that is given to him to finish the task. As people who are sent by God, we must also discern the time we are living in, concerning the important commission God has given us.

Let us look at some verses and understand the mystery hidden in them. We will first look at two references from the Gospel of John. One is in the story of the blind and the other is in the story of Lazarus.

> John 9:4-5 *⁴I must work the works of Him who sent Me while it is day; the night is coming when no one can work. ⁵As long as I am in the world, I am the light of the world.*

Is Jesus' statement really relevant to the disciples' question?

At first glance, it does not seem to be relevant because it is not a direct answer to the question. I have read this story thousands of times as a part of my spiritual discipline. Recently, during one of my Vigil Nights*, the Holy Spirit shook my heart while reading the Gospel of John, stopping me deeply in these verses. And for the first time, I could see that this verse was a very mysterious verse. Usually, I had read this story casually, but when the Holy Spirit opened my eyes, I discovered that Jesus' reply was truly relevant to the question of the disciples. I continued to read the Gospel of John, and to my astonishment, I found the same principal in the story of Lazarus.

> John 11:9-11 *⁹Jesus answered, "Are there not twelve hours in the day? If anyone walks in the day, he does not stum-*

---

* A night of prayer : the early fathers spent at least a night every week reading the Gospels in a prayerful way. One does not sleep but continues to pray all night, usually Saturday/Sunday, to receive the power of resurrection each week.

ble, because he sees the light of this world. ⁱ⁰ But if one walks in the night, he stumbles, because the light is not in him." ⁱⁱ These things He said, and after that He said to them, "Our friend Lazarus sleeps, but I go that I may wake him up."

The situation here was centered on whether or not Jesus should visit Lazarus. But Jesus answered in a seemingly irrelevant way. At that time, the Lord began to explain to me these verses and open my eyes on a prophetic message. What happened later in my country was proof of what I received, but this message is also intended for the whole body of Christ. The message is this: *a night shall come when no one can work, let us therefore work during the day, and exert all our effort before the night comes. Let us also prepare ourselves well for the night that is to come.*

Expanding on the initial statement Jesus made to his disciples, let us look at the whole story in order to understand these mysterious words of Jesus. First, let us go deep into the story of the man who was born blind.

John 9:1-6 *¹ Now as Jesus passed by, He saw a man who was blind from birth. ² And His disciples asked Him, saying, "Rabbi, who sinned, this man or his parents, that he was born blind?" ³Jesus answered, "Neither this man nor his parents sinned, but that the works of God should be revealed in him. ⁴I must work the works of Him who sent Me while it is day; the night is coming when no one can work. ⁵As long as I am in the world, I am the light of the world." ⁶When He had said these things, He spat on the ground and made clay with the saliva; and He anointed the eyes of the blind man with the clay.*

After His reply to the disciples, Jesus started to work. He spat on the ground and began to deal with the man's blind eyes. If Jesus' purpose was just to answer the question of the disciples, He would have answered in a straightforward way, *Neither this man nor his parents sinned,* and then would have dealt directly with the blind eyes. However, Jesus did not do this.

Therefore, we must notice that the actual purpose and focus here was not to clarify whether there was any sin connected to the man or his parents. If Jesus intended to answer the disciples about the man's sin, the verses would have been ordered differently - After verse 3, verse 6 would directly come next. It seems that verses 4 to 5 are interrupting the flow the story. This means that Jesus had another purpose, another message that He wanted to convey to the disciples. When we read this passage we usually think that verses 4 and 5 are just casual words in between brackets, but actually, they are Jesus' core message to his disciples.

We must remember that Jesus selected this small group of disciples for a purpose. They were first disciples of John the Baptist, who was a great teacher, and Jesus Himself discipled them after that. We must also take note of the fact that these passages in chapter 9 are of the final phase of Jesus' ministry on earth. This means that these disciples had been taught by John the Baptist, and then Jesus for about three years - thus very well trained.

However, Jesus surprises them with a matter of great importance, as if He was saying to them that He was not so pleased with their question. He was telling them that the issue was not about who sinned or the cause of blindness. According to Jesus, the issue was: knowing who is the one who is truly blind.

This was a big surprise for the disciples and it may be a big surprise for us today. Jesus desired to draw the attention of the disciples to a condition of inner blindness in their own sight; a blindness that is more serious than any physical blindness. It was as if Jesus was telling them; *it is not important to be preoccupied with the blindness of this man. What is important is to realize your own sight, whether you are suffering from your own inner blindness.* This was the reason for adding these statements in verses 4 and 5.

It is important to understand what is in the mind of the Lord. What is the blindness that Jesus wanted to draw attention to? When we understand the answer to this question, we can then understand what Jesus meant when He said, *I must work the works of Him who sent Me while it is day; the night is coming when no one can work.* Jesus wanted to draw attention to their inner blindness that hindered them from discerning the time.

Because of electricity, which is indeed a blessing, we have lost the value and significance of the distinction between day and night, and the difference between them. We are able to perform any type of work by day or by night; either by sunlight or by the artificial light of electric lamps. But try to imagine how different our lives would be if we had no light available during the night. If this were the case, we would live by a completely different schedule during the day. We would be so eager to finish one job after the other, and to be done before the night falls. It would have inevitably changed the schedule and program of our lives.

We must remember that we are sent and our purpose revolves around the key words, *work the work of Him who sent Me.* We are sent, and we are missionaries. Are we able to understand the work that is given to us, and how much time each of us has on earth to complete this task? It is unfortunate that most people are not even aware of the fact that each person has been given a special task and a set time to complete it. Because of this we often wander around different ministries without a clear focus.

Therefore, we must clearly understand what our individual tasks in the Kingdom are, and the time available to finish that task. Without truly understanding and discerning the main, special task God has given to us, we will not know where to go and what to do within the appointed time. This is because we are not yet commissioned. We must receive the Lord's words about the task we need to complete in order to be commissioned for the blessing of this generation.

There is a story of a spiritual father who lived and died during this generation. He lived with his disciples in a monastery in England. He had deep spiritual teachings and was well known during his time. He received many people, healing, teaching them, and counseling them in the ways of God. He was doing many blessed things. And then one day he surprised his disciples by asking them to prepare a tomb for him. He told them that he had finished his task and his life was soon coming to an end. His disciples did not understand what their teacher was saying. He surprised them even more when he told them that he had even finished his prayers. He said, "I brought to the Lord everything that I had to bring to Him in prayers and have fully finished my task. And because I do not belong to the earth, I must go back to my home." It was a matter of about two weeks when he really left to be with the Lord.

Do you think we could do this? Can we prepare a tomb for ourselves? Can anyone say with such certainty that he has completed his task? Has anyone even begun to fulfill his task?

When a student enters a university, he is given many books to study, he takes examinations, and after completing the program he finally receives a certificate of graduation. There is a beginning, a journey, and an end. If the physical life goes through these types of regular steps, how much more must the spiritual life go through these different steps; receiving the task, working to finish the task, and reaching the completion. Because of our inner blindness it is hard for us to discern these things, and thus, many are not entrusted with the responsibility for this generation.

I remember the time when I first received the call to be entrusted for the generation. It was a time that completely changed my life. It caused a deep change in my spiritual life that brought a new lifting up. I was traveling in an airplane, reading in my seat, when my inner eyes were opened to understand that He is waiting for those who are ready to receive a commission; a task for the generation. Then everything became very clear and definite. The reasons for all my work were now very clear, and I was going to different places to do something definite, and I knew that God's hand was empowering my work.

When the Holy Spirit opens up the inner sight He brings a clearer and deeper level of understanding concerning the responsibility for this generation. It is not a casual ministry; it is not teaching or evangelizing; it is something different that cannot be taught by others.

Only when God opens our eyes, will we be able to truly understand what being responsible for the generation means. Then we will be able to receive a definite task from God. It is different from person to person, but with this task we will receive a new anointing.

When we go to heaven we will discover many things. We will find many people there, blessed in the perfect presence of God. And the angels will bring forward the main thing that each person did on earth. And then we will see that one person had perhaps ministered in Korea, or Japan, another had an important role in China, another was a wonderful teacher, this person ministered to the youth, one was a wonderful preacher, and so on. And then there will be the person who was entrusted for the generation; who had a heart for his generation. Because of this, he was actually able to minister in all these different ministries. Those who had a heart for their generation were not interested in garnering a powerful ministry, nor to become anointed, or be well known by name, and not interested in having a big Church, but on the contrary, they were happy to be hidden, to simply bear the responsibility of bringing blessings to their generation.

> Isaiah 49:1-2 *¹ Listen, O coastlands, to Me, and take heed, you peoples from afar! The Lord has called Me from the womb; From the matrix of My mother He has made mention of My name. ² And He has made My mouth like a sharp sword; In the shadow of His hand He has hidden Me, and made Me a polished shaft; In His quiver He has hidden Me.*

The prophet Isaiah was speaking about a great man of God who was called from the womb of his mother, but said that he was hidden in the quiver. It is important to understand what our task is and to discern the time of day, because the night is coming soon. How can we do this? We can find the answer in John 5:19-20.

> John 5:19-20 *¹⁹ Then Jesus answered and said to them, "Most assuredly, I say to you, the Son can do nothing of Himself, but what He sees the Father do; for whatever He does, the Son also does in like manner. ²⁰ For the Father loves the Son, and shows Him all things that He Himself does; and He will show Him greater works than these, that you may marvel."*

Jesus was in a daily fellowship with His Father to perform the works of Him, who sent Him. Christ is our example, and exemplifies our responsibility to maintain a close fellowship with the Father, so that we may know the purpose and the task we must complete.

> 2 Corinthians 6:1 *We then, as workers together with Him also plead with you not to receive the grace of God in vain.*

This verse tells us that we are workers, working together with Him. The days and hours pass us by, while we are preoccupied with useless, silly things. We will not be able to bring back the day that is gone, and we will also have to give account for it.

Ephesians 5:16-17 *¹⁶ redeeming the time, because the days are evil. ¹⁷ Therefore do not be unwise, but understand what the will of the Lord is.*

This depends on the degree of insight we have, therefore, we must continuously pray for the opening of our insight and for the ability to discern the time and hours.

Let us go back to the story of Lazarus. In John 11, Jesus decided to go back to Bethany after hearing of Lazarus' sickness, despite the fact that he had recently departed the area due to the increased persecution and opposition against Him from the Jews. Lazarus' sisters sent for Jesus, telling Him that Lazarus was about to die and so they needed Him to come back. Jesus decided to go back to Bethany. The disciples were disturbed by this decision and began to object, "Rabbi, lately the Jews sought to stone You, and are You going there again?"

At first glance, the objection seems to be justified because it was true that the chief priest had given a direct command that anyone who knew where Jesus was should let them know so that He could be arrested. The disciples were implying that He must not go back there and that His decision was wrong. In this manner, the disciples spoke against their teacher's decision. They did this because they had in fact lost their inner sight. Jesus answered them again in a surprising and seemingly irrelevant way to bring to light the disciples' inner blindness.

> John 11:9-10 ⁹*Jesus answered, "Are there not twelve hours in the day? If anyone walks in the day, he does not stumble, because he sees the light of this world.* ¹⁰*But if one walks in the night, he stumbles, because the light is not in him."*

These disciples were trembling, tense, and they were only thinking of their own safety. The disciples had followed their teacher, thinking that He was a great man, and the One who would lead Israel to freedom from the Romans. They had hoped that Jesus would be the powerful king and they would be his close ministers. Now, they were afraid for His life, and if He was in danger, they knew that they would also be in danger. Therefore, they felt that they must keep Jesus away from the danger because this would also in turn assure their own safety.

But Jesus knew their hearts and thoughts and replied in this specific way to reveal to them an important message. Jesus was saying that this way of thinking by the disciples was not suitable for the children of God, more so, because they had only a few days ago finished talking about the previous event of the blind man, and yet stumbled again. This situation again had to do with the same principal of 'day and night.' It was as if Jesus was saying to them that the disciples' way of thinking not only reflected their inner blindness, but also reflected their ignorance of the reality of God as the one who controls everything.

Jesus was telling them that there are hours of work for each person. And each person has a time in which he works when no one can harm him. To be entrusted with the task of the responsibility for the generation, we must understand and have the assurance that we have a day of work when no one can harm us. It is related to the real task of the Kingdom of God; the real task that God has released to every person.

There are two portraits of those living for the Kingdom of God. In the example of the university student, there is the student who browses around in engineering, science, math, or English, here and there, not focused on any one thing in particular. He is not enrolled in one major and does not go through examinations, but he is just enjoying himself, reading a little bit here, and attending some other lecture there. And, there is the dedicated student who is perhaps studying commerce, with a goal of five textbooks to complete, and with the full awareness of the exam coming up next September. This student has a definite task and a definite timeline. We must remember that there are days and hours to finish the definite and specific task.

> Luke 13:32 *And he said to them, "Go and tell that fox, Behold, I cast out demons and perform cures today and tomorrow, and the third day I shall be perfected."*

Herod had a message delivered to Jesus; leave the country or face death. But Jesus replied in Luke 13:32, that Herod could not harm Him until His task had been completed. Peter also speaks about this protection;

> 1 Peter 3:13-14 *[13] And who is he who will harm you if you become followers of what is good? [14] But even if you should suffer for righteousness' sake, you are blessed. "And do not be afraid of their threats, nor be troubled."*

When you read the Gospel of John, you will find that Jesus repeats a single word many times. This word is *hour*, or *time*.

From the start of Jesus' ministry when He turned water into wine in Cana, Galilee, at His mother's request, He replied that his hour had not yet come. This was a mysterious thing, because Jesus was not referring to the matter of the wine, but was referring to the hour, the hour of the cross, where He would give mankind the real wine they needed, which was the Holy Spirit. However, that outpouring of the Holy Spirit could not be made available until the task of the cross was completed, and the time had not yet come.

Jesus was not afraid of the cross, and knew the price, and as Paul says in Hebrews; there was a pleasure behind the sacrifice of the cross, which was the salvation of humanity. Jesus continued to repeat this phrase throughout the last part of the Gospel of John; *My hour has not yet come.* And finally, at the end of His ministry, Jesus completed everything with His intercessory prayer in chapter 17. The first words he prayed were, *Father the hour has come* (John 17:1).

In the three Gospels that record the crucifixion, it says that the soldiers bound His hands. These were the hands that touched people with healing and deliverance, and yet they became bound, unable to touch the people anymore. Jesus had already finished His work on earth, and that is why they were able to bind Him. Jesus had finished His good works and He was going to the cross for the eternal good of our salvation.

This whole portrait reveals to us that every person has a

day; an hour. And the night is coming soon, all over the world. This night is a spiritual night in which no one can work. I assure you that the time will come when books such as these, seminars, conferences, gatherings, or even speaking the name of Jesus will be forbidden, and people will even be unable to pray in their own homes or repent.

Have we prepared ourselves for all the possibilities that can come with this night? Have we filled our lamps with oil? Have we thought of those who need to be saved, those around us in our generation that we live in? Are we vigilant and watchful so that our deposit of grace may increase and be sufficient for the confrontations that are coming in the night to this generation?

Please thoughtfully pray and wrestle over these questions, and find your strength in the Lord.

Ephesians 6:10 *Finally, my brethren, be strong in the Lord and in the power of His might.*

II

HOW CAN WE BE RESPONSIBLE FOR THE GENERATION?

How can we be responsible for the generation? Let us look through Scripture in order to understand this question clearly and biblically.

> Psalm 89:19-21 [19] *Then You spoke in a vision to Your holy one, and said: "I have given help to one who is mighty; I have exalted one chosen from the people.* [20] *I have found My servant David; With My holy oil I have anointed him, with whom My hand shall be established; Also My arm shall strengthen him."*

In this passage, it seems that God is searching for a person; *I have found my servant in David.* We can see that God is searching to find a chosen vessel. He will pour the oil of the Holy Spirit on him. Not only this, God will release His arm and His power to be with this person. There is additional testimony of God concerning David also in the New Testament.

> Acts 13:22 *And when He had removed him, He raised up for them David as king, to whom also He gave testimony and said, 'I have found David the son of Jesse, a man after My own heart, who will do all My will.'*

In both the Old Testament and the New Testament, David is described as a chosen vessel; God was pleased with him and anointed him.

We can find another chosen vessel in Acts 9:15-16; this man is Paul.

> Acts 9:15-16 *[15] But the Lord said to him, "Go, for he is a chosen vessel of Mine to bear My name before Gentiles, kings, and the children of Israel. [16] For I will show him how many things he must suffer for My name's sake."*

From these verses we can find the answer to the question: who is to be entrusted and set apart to serve the generation? The one that can be entrusted to serve the generation should be a chosen vessel who has received a spiritual anointing, which then qualifies him to serve the generation.

For this anointing, a person first needs to know the characteristics and the main features of his generation. Every one of us is actually a part of the generation that we live in and so we must find these characteristics and features of the generation within ourselves; these may be weaknesses or difficulties. We must also understand the plan of God to deal with these weaknesses or problems of the generation.

FOUR
Understanding the main features and characteristics of the generation

What is the plan and the economy of the Holy Spirit for this generation?

First, it is important to know that God controls everything and directs everything in the direction of His will, because God has definite purposes and goals He wants to achieve. It is also important to know that God not only controls matters related to the Church, but also matters related to the nations and the governments. This is very clear in the book of Daniel. God directs everything in spiritual directions toward His plans and goals because God is preparing all the generations toward one final goal; the second coming as the King.

But at the same time, the enemy, who always works to

oppose and hinder God's plan, is cunningly pushing everything in the opposite direction. God is pushing everything towards one direction, but the enemy is continually pushing from the opposite direction. What can we expect from such a situation? Mechanically speaking, when a force meets an opposing force, the force can no longer stay on its path, but deviates.

Unfortunately, this happens all the time. And so, the responsibility of the Church of God and the children of God is to understand the mechanical outcome of this opposition, to constantly realign the deviated direction, and to make it come back into its proper path, so that the path reaches its destination and final purpose of His second coming. It is a reality that the enemy is pushing the whole dynamics of the world into the direction of hindering and blocking His second coming, because the enemy knows that when Jesus comes, he will be condemned in the fire. Unfortunately, most of us do not understand all these things.

If you follow the statistics and results of the activity of the Church of God, you will know that a lot of things are done with a tremendous amount of effort, but in the meantime, the Church of God is moving downward, going downhill, and the spirit of the world in entering the Church. The Church is embracing many ugly things. Many ministers and servants are still entering the Church to serve, but the spirit of the world is also entering deeper and deeper into the Church.

Why is this happening? It is because we minister, but minister blindly. Our ministries do not share in God's special goals; they are misaligned, and do not realign because we cannot even see the deviation. If we understand the deviation, then we can answer this question regarding each ministry; does this ministry help in realigning the direction of God's work towards His purpose? If the answer is no and it is not realigning, we can choose not to share in this ministry.

In Hebrews 1:2, it says that *He made the worlds*. The original Greek word for *made* is *fashioning*. We need to *refashion* this generation. Fashion means a special pattern in God's mind, according to which He made the whole world. However, this fashion is distorted and we need to realign, to refashion it again to come back to His pattern.

> Romans 12:2 *And do not be conformed to this world, but be transformed by the renewing of your mind.*

When reading the word of God, we are all prone to this problem; we tend to focus on one part of the verse and neglect the other part. In this particular verse, we often focus on the part of transforming and renewing of our minds, while neglecting the first part, which is so important; *do not be conformed to this world.* This tells us that every generation has a special *form*, and Paul is admonishing us to not be *conformed*, or take the form of the generation that we live in.

But this means that we must first discern the form of our generation so that we may flee from it. If we are not warned that the food placed in front of us is poisoned, we will eat it. Who would ignore the warning of the poisoned food?

In the same way, Paul warns us to take care, because there is a form around us and this form is wrong, thus we must not conform to it. In order to avoid this form, Paul says to renew our minds by the word of God, which brings light into our inner eyes, and then we can see what the form of this generation is. We will then be able to discover that this form is stamped in our lives and we can begin to push it away and begin to be cleansed of it. And then we will be transformed.

So, to be transformed, we must first know the form of the generation and then we must discover it in our own lives, and only then will we be really able to fight against it. For example, we are living in a generation that is very arrogant. We usually notice this arrogance in others first, and not in ourselves. We do not easily notice that we ourselves are also arrogant. First, we must see what the form of the generation is, but then we must also look within our own lives, and then we will soon be able to realize that we, too, are arrogant. Since it is already around us we can see that the people of our generation are very arrogant, and because we belong to the generation, this arrogance is actually also within us. And then, we must ask the Lord to cleanse us and humble our hearts.

We can see a clear biblical reference regarding this issue in the book of Isaiah.

Isaiah discovered the sickness of the generation inside himself

> Isaiah 6:5 *Woe is me, for I am undone! Because I am a man of unclean lips, and I dwell in the midst of a people of unclean lips; for my eyes have seen the King, The Lord of hosts!*

When Isaiah said these words, he had already finished much of the work of his ministry. This was in chapter 6, and so he had already finished 5 chapters of work. In the 5 chapters, he told of many things he did and preached to the people. However, he found that the people were unresponsive and became angry with them. He was angry because he had preached so much to them, yet they were not reacting to his message. In fact, within the first 5 chapters, the exasperated and enraged words, *woe to you* is used multiple times.

In light of this anger, Isaiah entered into a special season of retreat. He decided to go to the Lord to find the cause of the unresponsiveness of the people. He entered into the temple, knelt down to pray, and the Lord, in His mercy, came to him. Isaiah received a real and great vision, where he saw God on His throne with the angels surrounding Him saying, *Holy, Holy, Holy*. It was truly an encounter with the Holy God. From this encounter Isaiah discovered that not only were the lips of his generation defiled, but for the first time, he discovered that he shared the same problem; his own lips were also defiled.

Let us pause and think about this for a moment. A prophet with defiled lips! Isaiah had finished his task, a major part of his ministry in the first 5 chapters. Isaiah had the anointing of the prophet, and the word came to him from the Lord, which was released through his lips! But because his lips were defiled, the power of the words was lost. The word came to Isaiah in power, but passing through his defiled lips, it lost its power and when the people received the powerless words they did not respond. It was as if the people were hearing mere thoughts in their minds, with no power, and with no conviction; therefore, they did not repent. Isaiah, meanwhile, became angry and through his lips, repeated, *woe to you, woe to you.*

Then in the presence of the Lord, Isaiah realized that this was his fault, and he could now see things clearly. The light was upon him and his eyes were opened. The problem of the generation was a defiled life, but Isaiah understood that this was also his problem. He had defilement in his life, and so his ministry was powerless. He realized that if he wanted to minister to his generation, he had to begin with himself and deal with his own problem first; get his lips cleansed so that the power would not be lost. And then, he could go back to his generation, but this time he would be a different person, with cleansed lips and with empowered words. And because of this, his generation was able to repent and change.

> Isaiah 6:6-8 *⁶Then one of the seraphim flew to me, having in his hand a live coal which he had taken with the tongs from the altar. ⁷And he touched my mouth with it, and said: "Behold, this has touched your lips; your iniquity is taken away, and your sin purged." ⁸Also I heard the voice of the Lord, saying: "Whom shall I send, and who will go for Us?" Then I said, "Here am I! Send me."*

Here in verse 6, Isaiah received that cleansing with a

coal from the altar, and in verse 8, Isaiah said, *Lord, send me anew, send me again,* as if he had never been truly sent. Isaiah did not begin by asking the Lord to send him, but after being cleansed, he heard the voice of the Lord saying, *Whom shall I send?* And now, Isaiah was greatly broken, it was as if he was hearing God saying, "Isaiah, you have not been sent because you had no power, and all your past ministry was powerless. You were a prophet without power. I need to send a powerful prophet who must be cleansed from the sickness of the generation."

Isaiah received the message from God and understood Him. Isaiah received a new sending, a new anointing, and a new prophetic ministry. And because of this, Isaiah was even able to look sharply up to the day of Christ. As you know in Isaiah chapter 53, he spoke about the cross.

This is how to be entrusted for the generation, how to minister and how to be responsible for the generation. You must first discover the sickness of the generation. How can we discover it? We can discover it in our own lives. When Isaiah went into the presence of the Lord in the temple and encountered the Holy God, he could clearly see the bad things and stamps on his life and he cried, *cleanse me!* He knew from first glance that this was the sickness of his generation and that he was a part of the generation.

FIVE
Features and weaknesses of our generation

What are the dominant features of our generation? We are a part of the body of Christ. It does not matter whether we live in America, Egypt, or Korea, because we face the same enemy and we are a part of the same body of Christ. We have the same faith and the same goals. We are waiting for Christ to come again. We are all called to live a holy life. And because of this the enemy fights against us.

And so, we can also find the same general features in our generation. Of course, there are specific features that belong to different peoples and nations respectively, but there are main features belonging to all of us, not only because we face the same enemy, but because we all have the same weaknesses from our fallen nature. And when we receive the new nature, which is of Christ, then the fallen nature begins to surface as it clears up more and more.

That being said, these are the main features of our generation, but not the final conclusion. We can try to find more features within ourselves.

Uncleanliness and the absence of the fear of God

The people of the previous generation, 50 years ago for example (maybe you were part of this generation), were very different from us. They were more serious, more committed, and had a fear of God. Much more so than our generation. This is due to the defilement that came to our consciences.

> 2 Corinthians 6:17 *Come out from among them and be separate, says the Lord. Do not touch what is unclean, and I will receive you.*

Passions and lust

In this generation there is an absence of self-control and spiritual self-discipline; in girding our waist, and controlling ourselves. Self-discipline or spiritual discipline was not lightly regarded in the early centuries of the Church. In the early centuries, every believer coming to Christ, learned how to go through daily spiritual disciplines. He learned how to pray regularly, to read the Bible regularly, more than one times a day, to fast regularly, and learned the biblical principles behind each of these aspects.

However, because of the loss of self-control through the generations, we began to look at these spiritual disciplines as though they were the law of the Old Testament, related to legalism, and old-fashioned. Now, we usually think that living by the Spirit means that we are free of any law, and that we can casually pray anytime throughout our day, and that we do not need a separate and regular prayer time. If we cannot find prayer time, we do not consider it a big deal, because we are in the Spirit and we are not under any obligations. We mean good things, but we are very confused. What we are not able to understand is that these are not obligations, and of course, we are free of any law, but these are the controls of love; things that control a person who loves God; expressions of love; a response of the believer for a lover.

There has been much scholastic work done in recent years on the Old Testament, showing us that even the law of the Old Testament was not as we previously thought, but it was God asking his people to respond to Him and His love. He showed love, but desired self-control in our response back to Him. In the last 25 years a great deal of biblical research has been done in Europe and in the U.S. to prove these things and to correct the misunderstanding brought about in the Middle Ages and the Reformation regarding legalism.

Even when Adam was created, God placed a condition before him: *but of the tree of the knowledge of good and evil you shall not eat.* Adam could eat from every tree but one. In the same way, God desires us to put ourselves through a girding process with these spiritual disciplines. If we lose these disciplines, we lose the fear of God, lose our self-control, and we will easily be overcome by lust and bad passions. These become a stumbling block for many people. It gives opportunity to the devil to whisper in our ears; "there is no victory, it is too difficult."

Disappearance of deep faith and patience

Instead of having faith and waiting patiently upon the Lord, we see in this generation a tendency towards rushing, hastening, and seeking prestige for oneself (Hebrews 6:12).

Absence of a sacrificial life

Matthew 20:28 *just as the Son of Man did not come to be served, but to serve, and to give His life a ransom for many.*

Philippians 1:29 *For to you it has been granted on behalf of Christ, not only to believe in Him, but also to suffer for His sake.*

Philippians 3:10 *that I may know Him and the power of His resurrection, and the fellowship of His sufferings, being conformed to His death.*

God's true and genuine calling requires self-denial. More than that, it requires an acceptance of suffering for Christ. Suffering in itself is a gift, and it is a path toward the power of resurrection. In Greek, the word *granted* has the meaning of *gifting* or *giving*, and thus God is giving us, entrusting us with a gift of the fellowship of Christ's sufferings.

Excessive talking, making human plans, and wisdom of the flesh, instead of the wisdom of God

1 Corinthians 1:30 *But of Him you are in Christ Jesus, who became for us wisdom from God - and righteousness and sanctification and redemption.*

James 3:17 *But the wisdom that is from above is first pure, then peaceable, gentle, willing to yield, full of mercy and good fruits, without partiality and without hypocrisy.*

SIX
Remedies to help
with the weaknesses of our generation

When Isaiah discovered the problem of his generation, he also found what God had prepared for him. Isaiah went to the temple seeking God, and God opened his eyes to see his problem and the problem of the generation. God did not just leave Isaiah after that. God was also preparing the remedy. He was preparing for him the charcoal with the seraphim to serve him.

We have already reviewed the main features of this generation, and of course these features must also be discovered in our own lives. But we must also have the corresponding remedy; the corresponding salvation. There are three things, remedies that will help with the weaknesses of our generation: the icon, spiritual inheritance and prayer.

Icon*

This generation has become so satisfied with what they hear, read, and know. There are so many spiritual books, meetings, conferences, and speakers. We hear and read a great deal, yet we lack victory, holiness, and we do not live a real Christian life. This is because we lack an important thing; the Christian life is not just about hearing and reading, it must also be seen.

We need examples; people living a holy life, and shining with the grace of Christ. In previous generations we could find many people with these characteristics, even though they did not have many books or conferences available to them. We need to live deeply in Christ. Instead of devoting our time to gatherings, or activities, we must take part of this time and really pull ourselves in front of Him. We have to spend enough time in our temples like Isaiah. We need to encounter a Holy God, to receive holiness. I know that the grace of salvation has holiness in it, because Christ has made us holy in Him, but we need to be able to release His holiness.

---

* Icon is a word, which describes a religious picture, used to depict the image of God. The word is derived from the Greek *eikon* or the Coptic word *eikonigow*. It is used in Genesis 1:26-27 in the Greek Bible; *Then God said, let us make man in our image..., so God created man in His own image, in the image of God he created.* This word is also used in Colossians 1:15 in the Greek Bible, *He is the image of the invisible God.*

As the Bible says, we need to be a living icon. In this way, when people meet us or talk to us, they will be able to see that we are not ordinary, but that Christ is really living within us. As Paul said in Galatians 2:20, *it is no longer I who live, but Christ lives in me.* Paul was able to go through a series of self-denial and self-death. Paul learned the art of putting himself to death, so that Christ could live in him. He learned how to put to death his ego, his self, to create a room for Christ to come and dwell in him.

> John 14:23 *Jesus answered and said to him, "If anyone loves Me, he will keep My word; and My Father will love him, and We will come to him and make Our home with him."*

> Galatians 4:19 *My little children, for whom I labor in birth again until Christ is formed in you!*

> Ephesians 3:17 *that Christ may dwell in your hearts through faith; that you, being rooted and grounded in love.*

Christ desires to come and dwell literally within us; he must be formed within us and we need to turn into a living icon!

Spiritual Inheritance

In every country, there is a past inheritance passed down from the men of God who lived in the previous centuries. When a real man of God passes away, he leaves an inheritance behind him: his story, his relationship and dealings with God. For sure, there are men of God that lived in your respective countries in previous centuries and you may have some of their stories.

These stories should not be regarded as casual stories, merely to encourage us, because the work of the Spirit in a man of God cannot be abolished. It is an actual inheritance that we can receive into our own lives. When our fathers die, they leave an inheritance behind for us to receive. We inherit land or money. Our spiritual fathers also leave us with spiritual inheritance and blessings that we can receive in our lives.

In my early years as a brother, I remember reading the autobiographies of the spiritual fathers; on my knees, and soaked in tears. I said to the Lord, "Lord, you could not have brought me this history simply to amaze me, nor to make me jealous of them, but I am sure that you want to speak to me by saying that I can be like them, and to receive from them." They were not just men; they were men whom the Holy Spirit was present in them.

They have passed away from this world, but what the

Holy Spirit has done within them cannot pass away with them; it has been left for us to receive. We can receive their diligence and humbleness. And then, we can ask the Holy Spirit to give to us what was given to them. When a son comes to his father and says, "You gave my brother a lovely gift, and I would also like to have a gift just like him," the father would not refuse his son this gift. The Holy Spirit gave our brothers of the previous generation something precious, so we must kneel down, exercise our faith, and ask the Holy Spirit to give to us as He has given to the others in the past. We must pray, "I am also in need, maybe in need more than them!"

Remember Elisha who asked for double the spiritual blessings that had been given to Elijah, despite the fact that Elijah said it would be a difficult request. But the double portion was granted. Can you see the biblical principal here? Elisha, being the disciple of Elijah, saw many wonderful things done through Elijah. After Elijah departed, Elisha was not content to just talk about what he had witnessed or merely be encouraged by it. No, Elisha knew that he could also receive through these examples, because the One who gives is the same; the Spirit of God.

However, he needed the prayer of his spiritual father, so Elisha said, "Please Elijah, help me before you leave, I need double the portion of your spirit. My eyes are open and I can see that my generation needs a lot more than you. You opened the door for me, but I have a big task and I need a double portion of your spirit." And Elisha was granted!

Hebrews 13:7 *Remember those who rule over you, who have spoken the word of God to you, whose faith follow, considering the outcome of their conduct.*

Prayer and spiritual disciplines

Scripture and the early fathers have given us many great words about prayer. Whether we are in Church, at home, at work, traveling, or at leisure, prayer constitutes our most intimate union with God.

It is inconceivable even to imagine oneself as being a Christian without prayer. To walk with God's presence felt continually in one's heart is to walk with unceasing prayer. Christ Himself is our example who not only prayed corporally (Matthew 14:23; 26:36; Luke 6:12; John 17), but perpetually "beheld" within, God the Father (John 10:38).

Let us look to some of the sayings of the early fathers of the Church:

St. Tikhon of Zadonsk wrote:
As a bird without wings, as a soldier without arms, so is

a Christian without prayer.

We are like birds ever striving to fly to God and dwell in His joyful presence. And we are like soldiers battling the dark, evil powers, which tempt us and often cause us to fall; with the wings of prayer we can turn to God and with the arms of prayer we can be victorious.

What is prayer and why is it needed?

What then, is prayer? Prayer is the raising of the mind and heart to God in praise and thanksgiving to Him and in supplication for the good things that we need, both spiritual and physical. Prayers are spiritual because they are originally born in the (human) spirit and ripen there by the grace of the Holy Spirit. In their origin they (i.e. prayers, psalms, hymns, etc.) were purely spiritual and only afterwards came to be clothed in words and so assumed an oral form. (Bp. Theophan the Recluse)

When you read the Gospels, Christ speaks to you; when you pray, you are speaking to Him. The Bible should be read not just for analysis, but also as an immediate dialogue with the living Word Himself, to feed our love for Christ, to kindle our hearts with prayer and to provide us with guidance in our personal life. (St. Tikhon of Zodonsk)

When one reads the Holy Scriptures, one should apply everything to oneself and not to someone else. As a book uniquely inspired by God and addressed to each of the faithful personally, the Bible possesses sacramental power, transmitting grace to the reader, bringing him to a point of meeting and decisive encounter with God. (St. Mark the Monk)

How to pray and types of prayer

When you pray, try to let the prayer reach your heart; in other words, it is necessary that your heart should feel what you are talking about in your prayer, that it should wish for the blessing for which you are asking. Observe, during prayer, whether your heart is in accord with that which you are saying. (St. John of Kronstadt)

Remember that while you pray, God expects from you a positive answer to His question: "Do you believe that I can fulfill your prayer?" You must be able to answer from the bottom of your heart: "Yes, I believe, O God," and then you will be answered according to your faith. (St. John of Kponstodt)

How many times have I prayed for what seemed a good

thing for me and not leaving it to God to do as He knows best. But having obtained what I begged for, I found myself in distress because I had not asked for it to be, rather, according to God's will. (St. Nilus of Sinai)

Do not rush one prayer after another but say them with orderly deliberation, as one addressing a great person for a favor. Do not just pay attention to the words, but rather let the mind be in the heart, standing before the Lord in full awareness of His presence, in full consciousness of His greatness and grace and justice. (Theophan the Recluse)

I advise you to convince yourself and force yourself to prayer and every good action, even if you do not feel the desire for it. God seeing such labor and application will give you goodwill and zeal. Such good will and a certain attraction to prayer is often a result of habit. Get into this habit and it will draw you to prayer and good actions. (St. Tikhon of Zadonsk)

Pray without ceasing (1 Thessalonians 5:17)

Make sure that you do not limit your prayer merely to a particular part of the day. Turn to prayer at anytime. (St. John Chrysostom)

In everything they (the Apostles) did, they thought of

God and lived in constant devotion to Him. This spiritual state was their unceasing prayer. (St. Basil the Great)

Rising in the morning stand as firmly as possible before God in your heart, as you offer your morning prayers and then go to the work apportioned to you by God, without withdrawing from Him in your feelings and consciousness. (Bp. Theophan the Recluse)

Those who have truly decided to serve the Lord God should practice the remembrance of God and uninterrupted prayer to Jesus Christ, mentally saying: "Lord Jesus Christ, Son of God, have mercy on me a sinner." (St. Seraphim of Sarov)

Let not one think, my fellow Christian, that only priests and monks need to pray without ceasing and not laymen. No, no; every Christian without exception ought to dwell always in prayer. (St. Gregory Polomas)

III

HOW CAN WE BLESS OUR GENERATION?

In the previous chapters, we talked about how we can understand our responsibility for the generation. Now, we need to talk about how we can bless our generation. There are two main points that I would like to cover.

First, we should not use personal suggestions on how to bless this generation, but we must search the Scriptures to understand God's mind on this matter. When we talk about blessing the generation, we commonly bring our own suggestions and personal ideas to spiritual things. We must find the biblical basis on this subject.

Second, we must understand and consider the fact that our generation is the generation of the end times.

SEVEN
Searching the Scriptures to understand God's mind concerning the blessing of the generation

God's mind does not change. The pictures may vary, and the applications may take various forms according to the economy of the Holy Spirit, yet God's truth remains the same from one generation to the next.

The first man who was really blessed openly by God was Abraham. God worked with Abraham and blessed him, and Abraham became a blessing. All the scholars agree on one main principal concerning Bible teaching in general; that whenever we want to find a principal in Bible teaching, it is better to find the principal in the first five books of Moses. The first five books hold the main teachings of God to His people, Israel. In these books we find the principles of blessing through the life of Abraham; whom God blessed and made a blessing.

God's work with Abraham comprised of two main components: the promise and the covenant. The promise was spoken of in Genesis 12, and the covenant in Genesis 15 and 17. The covenant is such an important and foundational topic. Therefore, we will look deeply into the topic of the covenant and our covenant relationship with God in the last chapter of this book.

We must first understand that God desires us to be separate and set apart from the world. To receive God's promise and be a people of His covenant, we need to be "set apart."

> 2 Corinthians 6:14-7:1 *[14] Do not be unequally yoked together with unbelievers. For what fellowship has righteousness with lawlessness? And what communion has light with darkness? [15] And what accord has Christ with Belial? Or what part has a believer with an unbeliever? [16] And what agreement has the temple of God with idols? For you are the temple of the living God. As God has said: "I will dwell in them and walk among them. I will be their God, and they shall be My people." [17] Therefore "Come out from among them and be separate, says the Lord. Do not touch what is unclean, and I will receive you." [18] "I will be a Father to you, and you shall be My sons and daughters, says the*

Lord Almighty." ⁷:¹ *Therefore, having these promises, beloved, let us cleanse ourselves from all filthiness of the flesh and spirit, perfecting holiness in the fear of God."*

To be able to receive the promises of God, and to be a man or woman of promise, you need to be "set apart" for the Lord. God can entrust His people to be a people of promise, if they are "set apart" for Him. If we are living an earthly life and walking in the power of the flesh, then we cannot hope to receive real promises. This may be the reason that sometimes we hold onto a promise but do not see it realized in our lives. Promises can really happen and be realized in those who are living in the Spirit and separate for the Lord.

Titus 2:14 *who gave Himself for us, that He might redeem us from every lawless deed and purify for Himself His own special people, zealous for good works.*

Notice here the phrase, *His own special people.* The word *special people* in Greek means extraordinary people; extraordinary in the eyes of the people around them. People will look at him and say that he is special and extraordinary. People will be drawn to this person because he has a special and heavenly attractiveness. However, if we begin to resemble others living around us, we lose our heavenly attractiveness.

There is a magnetic power in those living in the heavenly realm. Paul, in Ephesians, wrote that we have been raised and seated with Christ, and when we are there, we acquire this magnetic power around us. And then we are sent to the world as missionaries, living as visitors and strangers, but with a magnetic medium and power around us - able to impact every person in our path. This magnetic power will not necessarily draw every person to Christ; in fact some may even flee from it. But the point of this magnetic power is that when it touches a person, he cannot remain in spiritual sleep anymore. He is awakened and shook up, and must answer in one of two ways: either "Yes," and follow Christ, or "No," and follow the enemy.

> 2 Corinthians 2:15-16 *¹⁵ For we are to God the fragrance of Christ among those who are being saved and among those who are perishing. ¹⁶ To the one we are the aroma of death leading to death, and to the other the aroma of life leading to life. And who is sufficient for these things?*

We must acquire the aroma of Christ. And when we have the aroma of Christ, people will no longer be able to sleep - people will be shaken and must decide either, with

Christ, or without. And because of this we are sent here in the world as strangers. Without this aroma we will be useless and without any effect. Elijah spoke to the people who were spiritually drowsy.

> 1 Kings 18:21 *And Elijah came to all the people, and said, "How long will you falter between two opinions? If the Lord is God, follow Him; but if Baal, follow him." But the people answered him not a word.*

In the Old Testament, God set apart the tribe of Levi to watch and keep vigil over God's Holies. In the New Testament, the whole Church is a spiritual tribe that is set apart for the Lord.

> 1 Peter 2:5-10 *⁵ you also, as living stones, are being built up a spiritual house, a holy priesthood, to offer up spiritual sacrifices acceptable to God through Jesus Christ. ⁶ Therefore it is also contained in the Scripture, "Behold, I lay in Zion A chief cornerstone, elect, precious, and he who believes on Him will by no means be put to shame." ⁷ Therefore, to you who believe, He is precious; but to those who are disobedient, "The stone which the builders rejected has become the chief cornerstone," ⁸ and "A stone of stumbling and a rock of offense." They stumble, being dis-*

obedient to the word, to which they also were appointed. ⁹ But you are a chosen generation, a royal priesthood, a holy nation, His own special people, that you may proclaim the praises of Him who called you out of darkness into His marvelous light; ¹⁰ who once were not a people but are now the people of God, who had not obtained mercy but now have obtained mercy.

The actions of not being set apart hinders the promises, because the spirit of the world will come into our lives. The Bible warns us many times of avoiding the spirit of the world.

James 4:4 *Adulterers and adulteresses! Do you not know that friendship with the world is enmity with God? Whoever therefore wants to be a friend of the world makes himself an enemy of God.*

1 John 2:15-17 *¹⁵ Do not love the world or the things in the world. If anyone loves the world, the love of the Father is not in him. ¹⁶ For all that is in the world - the lust of the flesh, the lust of the eyes, and the pride of life - is not of the Father but is of the world. ¹⁷ And the world is passing away, and the lust of it; but he who does the will of God abides forever.*

God's blessing for Abraham was based on two main components: the promise and the covenant. Now let us look at the covenant. God desires a person of faith who knows the promises, respects their conditions, and holds on to a vision of fulfillment. But He also desires a person of the covenant. The person of faith knows how to hold onto the promises and practice true faith that does not depend on sight. Similarly, a person of the covenant knows and realizes the privileges of the covenant, while also recognizing their responsibilities.

Like in any partnership, a covenant involves commitments. When two people agree to work in a company together, they each have commitments - it is the same for Christians because Christ has completed everything on our behalf - we have actually entered into the covenant as partners of the covenant. Thus, we have responsibilities and commitments. We have been justified by His grace, and this justification was free, but we are still required to bear the fruits of righteousness. Here are some biblical examples to understand this point.

> Philippians 1:11 *being filled with the fruits of righteousness which are by Jesus Christ, to the glory and praise of God.*

> Ephesians 5:8-10 *⁸For you were once darkness, but now you*

are light in the Lord. Walk as children of light ⁹ *(for the fruit of the Spirit is in all goodness, righteousness, and truth),* ¹⁰ *finding out what is acceptable to the Lord.*

We often think that everything is by grace and there is nothing else that we need to do because Christ has done everything on our behalf. This is true; grace is free. However, German theologian, Dietrich Bonhoeffer, said that grace is free but it is not cheap. We have responsibilities and we have to work out our salvation. We have to show the world, the fruits of grace coming out of our lives. Our responsibilities are so clearly written in 2 Peter 1:4-11.

> 2 Peter 1:4-11 ⁴ *by which have been given to us exceedingly great and precious promises, that through these you may be partakers of the divine nature, having escaped the corruption that is in the world through lust.* ⁵ *But also for this very reason, giving all diligence, add to your faith virtue, to virtue knowledge,* ⁶ *to knowledge self-control, to self-control perseverance, to perseverance godliness,* ⁷ *to godliness brotherly kindness, and to brotherly kindness love.* ⁸ *For if these things are yours and abound, you will be neither barren nor unfruitful in the knowledge of our Lord Jesus Christ.* ⁹ *For he who lacks these things is shortsighted, even to blindness, and has forgotten that he was*

*cleansed from his old sins. *[10]* Therefore, brethren, be even more diligent to make your call and election sure, for if you do these things you will never stumble;* [11] *for so an entrance will be supplied to you abundantly into the everlasting kingdom of our Lord and Savior Jesus Christ.*

Another example is Christ's resurrection. The power of Christ's resurrection is beyond our imagination. When Paul tried to express and describe the power of the resurrection, he was fighting for words. He was struggling with the linguistic boundaries to show us the greatness of the power of His resurrection.

Ephesians 1: 18-20 [18] *the eyes of your understanding being enlightened; that you may know what is the hope of His calling, what are the riches of the glory of His inheritance in the saints,* [19] *and what is the exceeding greatness of His power toward us who believe, according to the working of His mighty power* [20] *which He worked in Christ when He raised Him from the dead and seated Him at His right hand in the heavenly places.*

When Jesus was raised from the dead, the first words He spoke were, *I also send you*. But what happened after He said these words? He breathed on them saying, *Receive the*

Holy Spirit. Actually, He was breathing into them the power of the resurrection and newness of life. Now that we have learned about the greatness of His resurrection, we will be able to agree that we cannot be sent to bless this generation without receiving a new infilling of the Spirit and without the power of the resurrection.

> John 20:19-22 *[19] Then, the same day at evening, being the first day of the week, when the doors were shut where the disciples were assembled, for fear of the Jews, Jesus came and stood in the midst, and said to them, "Peace be with you." [20] When He had said this, He showed them His hands and His side. Then the disciples were glad when they saw the Lord. [21] So Jesus said to them again, "Peace to you! As the Father has sent Me, I also send you." [22] And when He had said this, He breathed on them, and said to them, "Receive the Holy Spirit."*

EIGHT
A generation of the end times

To understand and realize our responsibility toward the blessing of the generation, we need to bear in mind the distinct state of our generation. Our generation is in fact the generation of the end times. In the end times, we find evil, confusion, and lack of faith. There must be a special economy, a special plan of God to minister during these end times.

> Malachi 4:5 *Behold, I will send you Elijah the prophet before the coming of the great and dreadful day of the Lord.*

Here is one of the biblical references related to the end times. God says that he will send Elijah the prophet. The interpretation of this verse is not concerned with the physical coming of Elijah. In Luke 1:17 we can see the initial fulfillment of this prophecy in the ministry of John the Baptist.

> Luke 1:17 *He will also go before Him in the spirit and power of Elijah, 'to turn the hearts of the fathers to the children,' and the disobedient to the wisdom of the just, to make ready a people prepared for the Lord.*

There is a principal that scholars generally agree on concerning the prophecies of the Bible. Usually there is an initial fulfillment during the time of the prophet and his ministry. But the prophecy can also be found applied in other generations after the initial fulfillment.

Yet the final and complete fulfillment of any prophecy will be in the end times. So, for the prophetic verse of Malachi 4:5, we know that the initial fulfillment was in the person of John the Baptist and his ministry, but the final and complete fulfillment will occur in the end times. What is the plan of God and how can we minister in the end times? This is one of the important clues to understand how to ask and realize how to minister in the end times. It is not a matter of waiting for Elijah to come, but rather a matter of receiving the distinct anointing that Elijah, and John the

Baptist received. The point is not the actual persons of Elijah and John the Baptist, but it is the anointing that they both received.

So what is the mystery of this anointing? To minister effectively in the end times, we need to receive a special anointing according to this clue. Both prophets ministered in power. Elijah was able to restore Israel from the worship of Baal back to Jehovah again. John the Baptist was able to shake Israel to prepare the nation for the coming of Christ incarnate.

We are now living in a spiritually drowsy generation. We are living among sleepy people; their inner man is asleep. If we minister in the casual way we are used to, we will be speaking only to their minds. They will hear, but not understand or react properly. We need to shake them and awaken their inner man. It is not a matter of human gifts, and it is not even a matter of spiritual gifts, it is much more than that.

Therefore, we need to receive the special anointing. Specifically, the anointing which John the Baptist and Elijah both received. There is mystery in this anointing that enabled both prophets to minister in power. Both of these prophets ministered to a sleepy, drowsy people; a people who had drifted away. This means that they were actually ministering to those who were considered to be dead in spirit. Their anointing enabled them to bring life to dead people. The mystery of this anointing is this: *the power of the resurrection.*

Where is the biblical proof to this statement? Elijah and his disciple, Elisha, who received the same anointing from his spiritual father (when he threw the cloak on him), were both the only prophets who were able to raise the dead. Elijah raised the son of the widow of Sidon from the dead, and Elisha raised the Shunammite woman's son. We cannot find any other stories in the Old Testament of people being raised from the dead. However, it is well known that Christ alone has the power of resurrection. However, Christ's power of resurrection can work backwards in the Old Testament and can work forward in the New Testament and until His Second Coming, like all of the saving economies of Christ.

By looking at the characteristics and features of the life and ministry of Elijah, and those of John the Baptist, we will be able to learn the lessons that are necessary to minister to this generation.

Characteristics of the ministry of Elijah

Battling in spirit against evil powers

What are the lessons that can be learned from the ministry of Elijah? Before Elijah even began his ministry, he did something very important. He never moved at random, as we tend to do these days. He was living in the mountains, battling against the power of the enemy through prayer. After which, he moved forward to accomplish the required task. We do not know the background story or of Elijah's upbringing and we find his story beginning all of a sudden in 1 Kings chapter 17, coming from the mountains. He began there in the mountains praying, battling against the evil powers forcing Israel to drift away. He then came to the physical realm to accomplish great things. He killed 450 prophets of Baal; false prophets that were under the influence of evil powers.

However, Elijah knew that he first needed to finish the battle with the evil powers through prayer, before controlling the false prophets who were deceiving Israel. When he finished the battle, he went to confront the false prophets, was able to kill them, and then restore Israel. How can a single person confront 450 prophets and kill them? It would have been very easy for any one of the false prophets to jump on Elijah and kill him instead, but it seems that they were all paralyzed before Elijah. The false prophets were trembling before Elijah, and all he had to do was call them to come forward one by one as he slew each of them. These false prophets knew that the people of Israel had now turned toward Elijah and were now against them. They knew that they no longer had any influence over the people of Israel.

But the main point was that their unseen powers of evil had already been broken through Elijah's prayer. This is the same way we need to minister in this generation. There is a spiritual battle we need to finish. There is deception and a lot of drifting away, everyone desiring to go according to one's own thoughts. We need to direct them back to the word of God, back to the Living God and our Savior. They must be freed from these deceptive powers. We cannot finish this battle without the power of the resurrection, and without receiving the anointing that Elijah and John the Baptist received.

Building the altar of prayer

There is another lesson that we need to learn from the ministry of Elijah. Elijah built the ruined and broken altar.

> 1 Kings 18:30-32 *³⁰ Then Elijah said to all the people, "Come near to me." So all the people came near to him. And he*

repaired the altar of the Lord that was broken down. ³¹ And Elijah took twelve stones, according to the number of the tribes of the sons of Jacob, to whom the word of the Lord had come, saying, "Israel shall be your name." ³² Then with the stones he built an altar in the name of the Lord; and he made a trench around the altar large enough to hold two seahs of seed."

Elijah was able to rebuild the altar of Israel. In the book of Exodus chapter 29, we read about this altar. It has an important characteristic.

Exodus 29:38-43 *³⁸ Now this is what you shall offer on the altar: two lambs of the first year, day by day continually. ³⁹ One lamb you shall offer in the morning, and the other lamb you shall offer at twilight. ⁴⁰ With the one lamb shall be one-tenth of an ephah of flour mixed with one-fourth of a hin of pressed oil, and one-fourth of a hin of wine as a drink offering. ⁴¹ And the other lamb you shall offer at twilight; and you shall offer with it the grain offering and the drink offering, as in the morning, for a sweet aroma, an offering made by fire to the Lord. ⁴² This shall be a continual burnt offering throughout your generations at the door of the tabernacle of meeting before the Lord, where I will meet you to speak with you. ⁴³ And there I will meet with* the children of Israel, and the tabernacle shall be sanctified by My glory.

Notice that two burnt offerings were given every day: one in the morning and one in the afternoon. Not only were two offerings given every day, but the fire was never to be quenched. God told Moses that whenever there was fire on the altar, Israel would be kept in peace and under protection. When the fire was extinguished, they would be in danger.

We need to learn the same lesson from that generation. We are now in the New Testament but we still need to build altars in our own homes. Our altars should be unseen, spiritual altars, but real altars. It is an altar because we have to make offerings upon it. These offerings are our prayers, and they must be regular. This means that the fire of our altars will not be quenched. Whenever we have altars in our homes, we are in peace and under His protection, and we can have a magnetic field around us. We are also called to offer sacrifices on the altar.

This is also referenced in the New Testament.

> Hebrews 13:15 *Therefore by Him let us continually offer the sacrifice of praise to God, that is, the fruit of our lips, giving thanks to His name.*

We have already read in 1 Peter 2:5 that we are a holy priesthood to offer spiritual sacrifices. If we are going to minister to and bless this generation, we must always have behind us, in our homes, an altar that is continuously on fire. If the fire on our altar is quenched, or if our altar is ruined or broken, we will be powerless and unable to receive the anointing of Elijah. We will not be able to shake the dead inner man of this generation, and our words will just be empty words without power.

Acquiring a daring faith

The third lesson from the ministry of Elijah is: we must acquire a "quality faith," the faith despite the apparent opposition.

> 1 Kings 18:41-45 *[41] Then Elijah said to Ahab, "Go up, eat and drink; for there is the sound of abundance of rain." [42] So Ahab went up to eat and drink. And Elijah went up to the top of Carmel; then he bowed down on the ground, and put his face between his knees, [43] and said to his servant, "Go up now, look toward the sea." So he went up and looked, and said, "There is nothing." And seven times he said, "Go again." [44] Then it came to pass the seventh time, that he said, "There is a cloud, as small as a man's hand, rising out of the sea!" So he said, "Go up, say to*

Ahab, 'Prepare your chariot, and go down before the rain stops you.'" ⁴⁵ Now it happened in the meantime that the sky became black with clouds and wind, and there was a heavy rain. So Ahab rode away and went to Jezreel.

There is a very important mystery within this passage. Elijah had dealt with the false prophets, shaking the sleeping nation of Israel, and brought it back to the worship of the Living God. Now Elijah knew that the rain could come down, because according to the law of Moses in the book of Deuteronomy, the rain would stop when Israel sinned, but when they repented the rain would return. And Elijah was working on that principal of the law. Because Elijah knew that Israel was sinning, he was able to stop the rain. Now that he had dealt with all that was wrong, he knew that the rain could come.

In verse 41, Elijah addressed King Ahab, and told him to return to his home because the rain would soon fall. He told the king that he had already heard the sound of the coming rain. After he spoke to Ahab, he went to the mountain again and began to take the position of prayer, seriously and fervently, with his head between his knees, asking God to send the rain. Then he sent his disciple to look to the sky. The disciple returned to tell Elijah that there was nothing. Elijah had just told the king that he had heard the sound of rain!

Even after he prayed, the disciple saw nothing in the sky. Elijah had heard the sound of the rain, then why was the sky so clear? It was because Elijah's senses and his ears were now working not in the physical realm but in the spirit realm. He could hear things happening in the spirit realm while the physical sky was still clear. Elijah continued to pray seven times and each time he sent his disciple out to see, whether there were any signs of rain. Six times the disciple came back to report that there were no signs of rain.

Most of us would be full of despair after the second or third time, and would turn against God, probably crying out something like, "Where are you God! Work for your name! The king will dishonor you if you don't make this happen!" Actually, the anger in us will be for the sake of our own honor and our own name, and God cannot be fooled.

Because we do not have the anointing Elijah received, our faith is limited. Elijah acquired the faith that could stand against opposition until he reached a real point of breakthrough. In verse 44, on the seventh time, the disciple came back to report a small cloud. A small cloud is expected to bring only a few drops of rain. But again, Elijah exercised the power of faith; even though it was still a small cloud, he sent his disciple to the king again to tell him to hurry; otherwise he would be prevented from reaching his home because of the rain. A small cloud can either be cleared up soon or send only a few drops of rain. How could Elijah dare to say these things when there was only a small cloud? It was because Elijah had a powerful faith, a daring faith, which was a result of his anointing. And in verse 45, we find that the rain was so heavy!

Paul describes this daring faith in Romans 4:17 from the life and experience of Abraham.

> Romans 4:17 *as it is written, "I have made you a father of many nations" in the presence of Him whom he believed - God, who gives life to the dead and calls those things which do not exist as though they did.*

Abraham was able to call things which did not exist as though they did. This is daring faith. We also need to acquire such a faith. We cannot bless our generation without learning these lessons - battling in the spirit against evil powers, building our altar of prayer with a constant flame, and acquiring this daring faith: all of these components are incorporated in the anointing of Elijah. We need to ask the Lord to send us again the anointing of Elijah to be able to minister and bless this generation in the end times.

Characteristics of the ministry of John the Baptist

Vision

Mark 1:2-4 *² As it is written in the Prophets: "Behold, I send My messenger before Your face, Who will prepare Your way before You." ³ "The voice of one crying in the wilderness: 'Prepare the way of the Lord; Make His paths straight.'" ⁴ John came baptizing in the wilderness and preaching a baptism of repentance for the remission of sins.*

John the Baptist was a voice crying in the wilderness. Imagine how difficult this would be. Try to imagine yourself sent by God into the wilderness. Many of us pray, "Help me to know what country you want to send me to. Is it Japan, China, Indonesia, or perhaps the Middle East?" But try to imagine God saying to you, "I am sending you to the wilderness. Go there and preach my Gospel in the wilderness." You would probably question God, "To whom shall I minister to? To the wild animals? Could the lion hear me? Doubtless the lion would most likely devour me."

What do you think the difficulty would be if you were sent to the wilderness? Whatever the fear may be, thirst, loneliness, or physical hardship - these fears expose our main focus. Our main focus is usually on our own needs and we are not focused on His Kingdom. Instead our questions should be, "Lord why the desert? Who will listen, who will accept and receive?" Let your focus be outside of yourself.

John the Baptist knew quite well the difficult task of proclaiming the Gospel in the desert, with no one there to hear or accept. Yet, he knew that the truth could never be lost, that it could never die even if it was proclaimed in the desert. Spiritually speaking, Israel was like a desert at that time. But John the Baptist did not lose hope, and ministered to them as a voice in the wilderness, because he knew that the truth could never die.

And because of this, he shared these wonderful words in Luke 3:5, *Every valley shall be filled, and every mountain and hill shall be made low, and the crooked shall become straight, and the rough places shall become level ways.* We need to acquire this vision.

Message

John the Baptist's message was centered on one word: repentance. It is a renewed message that cuts down the heart and transforms the whole life by the power of the Holy Spirit. We must minister the word repentance to our generation. It is a word that must never die or get old.

Sacrifice

John the Baptist continued to speak the truth until the time that Herod killed him. And all of the historical accounts of John the Baptist say that even after his head was put on the plate and given to the dancing girl in Herod's palace, a voice still came from his head, saying again to the king that it was wrong to take the wife of his brother. Whether this story from the old legends is accurate or not, it remains an example of the truth coming alive. Whether we are dying or living, the truth we stand for will continue to work even after our death.

> Hebrews 11:4 ...*God testifying of his gifts; and through it he being dead still speaks.*

Can we acquire such a life? As the Psalmist said in Psalm 119:109, *My life is continually in my hand, yet I do not forget Your law.* This truth must go deep into our hearts and lives.

> Acts 20:24 *But none of these things move me; nor do I count my life dear to myself, so that I may finish my race with joy, and the ministry which I received from the Lord Jesus, to testify to the gospel of the grace of God.*

These were the great words of apostle Paul. What made Paul's ministry so extensive and effective was that he was ready to die for Christ anytime, every day. He was filled with the love of Christ, and so he was able to sacrifice his entire life for the Gospel. Paul's motivation to be *slaughtered as sheep* was driven by his love for Christ.

> Romans 8:35-39 [35] *Who shall separate us from the love of Christ? Shall tribulation, or distress, or persecution, or famine, or nakedness, or peril, or sword?* [36] *As it is written: "For Your sake we are killed all day long; we are accounted as sheep for the slaughter."* [37] *Yet in all these things we are more than conquerors through Him who loved us.* [38] *For I am persuaded that neither death nor life, nor angels nor principalities nor powers, nor things present nor things to come,* [39] *nor height nor depth, nor any other created thing, shall be able to separate us from the love of God which is in Christ Jesus our Lord.*

IV

RECEIVING A NEW FILLING AND ANOINTING OF THE HOLY SPIRIT

We need to receive a new filling of the Holy Spirit; a new empowering of the Spirit. This will bring us to a question; how can we really receive a new power, a new infilling of the Spirit? Unfortunately, sometimes we approach this in a casual and routine way. As if we can just come to the Lord and say, "Lord, help me to receive a new filling of the Spirit." Or, I may recall some verses in the book of Acts and pray accordingly, remembering the many instances in which the apostles received a new filling of the Holy Spirit - so we repeat the words, "Fill me anew," but this usually leads to nothing.

But, before we discuss the important principles to help us to be filled anew and receive the power of the Spirit in a new way, let us go through some references in the book of Acts. We know that the first infilling was on the day of Pentecost. We must ask ourselves, whether we are really connected to that day of Pentecost.

> Acts 2:1-4 *[1] When the Day of Pentecost had fully come, they were all with one accord in one place. [2] And suddenly there came a sound from heaven, as of a rushing mighty wind, and it filled the whole house where they were sitting. [3] Then there appeared to them divided tongues, as of fire, and one sat upon each of them. [4] And they were all filled with the Holy Spirit and began to speak with other tongues, as the Spirit gave them utterance.*

In chapter 4, we read about another infilling of the Holy Spirit.

> Acts 4:31 *And when they had prayed, the place where they were assembled together was shaken; and they were all filled with the Holy Spirit, and they spoke the word of God with boldness.*

The scholars tell us that nearly every chapter of the book of Acts stands for one year. So in chapter 4, it has been four years after the day of the Pentecost. After four years, the apostles were ready to receive a new infilling of the Holy Spirit. Again, it was a real infilling accompanied with visible signs. The place where they were staying was shaken. However, this infilling that happened after four years has a story. It happened when the official authorities of the temple arrested the apostles.

The apostles were interrogated by the high priest and his helpers, and were told that they must not speak about Jesus again. It was a difficult time filled with confrontation. The usual approach that a person of our generation would take is probably to resort to their intellectual abilities and try to convince them that they have to continue preaching. Many times, we depend on our own abilities when faced with confrontations. However, these apostles, only proclaimed the truth in front of the opposing people, and they were very calm but bold, and very true.

In verse 19, Peter and John simply said to them; *whether it is right in the sight of God to listen to you more than to God, you judge.*

After they had been released, they went back to their fellow apostles and shared their story with them. Now the whole group of the apostles, together, realized that they too were in need of a new infilling of the Holy Spirit. They were facing many difficulties, and knew that they could not depend on their own abilities or convictions. They realized that they could not defend the battle depending on their flesh. Therefore, from their hearts, they brought forward their real need to the Lord in prayer. And the Lord answered them through the pouring of the Holy Spirit, again in a very powerful way. And they received a new infilling of the Holy Spirit.

Again in Acts 13, Paul was faced with a new confrontation. It was not a confrontation with the authorities of the temple trying to stop the story of Jesus, but it was against a sorcerer who tried to confuse people. Paul knew that he was now face to face with the enemy, with the devil, represented by one of his servants of sorcery. We are able to see that Paul knew of his need in that moment for the new infilling of the Holy Spirit in order to be victorious in this battle.

> Acts 13:9 *Then Saul, who also is called Paul, filled with the Holy Spirit, looked intently at him.*

We cannot read about Paul's prayer for the infilling, but his heart was crying out for help. Heaven answered with the pouring of the Holy Spirit. Many times, we pray but do not receive such a power. We do not recognize that it is not a matter of words but a matter of a real heart crying out for a real need. Paul realized that we are all in need of a continuous infilling of the Spirit. When Paul wrote his epistle to the Ephesians, in chapter 5 verse 18, he used the continuous, present tense in Greek. At the end of the verse, *being filled with the Spirit,* actually means *being continually filled with the Spirit.*

NINE
Principles in receiving a new filling of the Holy Spirit

Now we come to an important question; how can we really be ready to receive a new filling of the Holy Spirit? We are speaking about a special type of filling that can prepare us and empower us to minister to the generation we are living in. There are 3 main principles needed in order to receive this new filling of the Spirit related to our generation: encountering the Holy God, restoring the original spring of the Pentecost, and responsibility toward the generation.

Encountering the Holy God

How can we encounter God as a Holy God? And why do I

use this term *Holy God* and not, for example, the *Living God*? The Bible reveals God in different ways, using different names like *Living God*, *Holy God*, or *God Almighty*. In Hebrew, there are about 8 different names for God. All the names of God reveal to us a truth that is to be practiced and applied. Truth not applied, is truth denied. Therefore, we need to encounter the Holy God. You will soon come to understand why we need that encounter with a Holy God. Before that, we need to ask the question, how can we come into that encounter with the Holy God?

This encounter takes place when one cries out in true need, feeling devoid of God's Life, feeling the inner emptiness, so he cries out, "God, come and fill me, I am empty, I am dry, I am ignorant, and I am a wretched man."

Remember Paul's statement in Romans 7:24, *O wretched man that I am! Who will deliver me from this body of death?* The answer to Paul's cry was in Romans 8:2; *for the law of the Spirit of life in Christ Jesus has made me free from the law of sin and death.* Paul received the Spirit of life.

Paul had cried out; *who will deliver me from this body of death,* and the answer was the Spirit of life. Against death, life! Against body, Spirit! The wonderful thing is that when we cry out to God, He does not answer us in words, but in action. He did not just tell Paul, "Ah yes, you need the Spirit of life." God actually gave Paul the Spirit of life, and Paul began to realize and experience the release of death.

> Revelation 3:17 *Because you say, 'I am rich, have become wealthy, and have need of nothing' - and do not know that you are wretched, miserable, poor, blind, and naked.*

The man in the verse was a bishop of a church in the area of Asia during the time of Apostle John. He was standing exactly in the contrary position to Paul. Paul was feeling his need, but this man was feeling no need for himself. Because of this, he could not find any help from the Lord. There was no place in his inner man to receive any pouring out from the Lord, and thus he received these warning words from Him, *You are wretched, miserable, poor, blind, and naked.* When Paul said, "I am wretched," God rescued him. When this man said, "I am okay, I have everything, I have need of nothing," the Lord said to him, "you are wretched."

When the Holy God appears before us, we are able to see ourselves in a different way. We can see ourselves through the eyes of the One to whom we must give account, the One who searches everything, even the hidden things of darkness.

1 Corinthians 4:5 *Therefore judge nothing before the time, until the Lord comes, who will both bring to light the hidden things of darkness and reveal the counsels of the hearts. Then each one's praise will come from God.*

We have often neglected and ignored the encounter with the Holy God and seeing ourselves through the eyes of the Holy God. We only focus on the Loving God. We always hear and speak about God's love but we rarely hear preaching or teaching about God's holiness. When a person comes to warn us, saying, "God is holy so we must take our life of faith seriously," we think to ourselves, "no, God is loving, God is forgiving!" We reach the point where we believe God only loves and can accept mistakes. As if, this loving God does not mind wrongdoings. We have this mindset because we are so absorbed in loving and pitying ourselves.

But history tells us that all the holy men of God, whether worshipers or ministers, living alone in the desert or living among people, performing miracles or releasing revivals; these people were the ones who knew how to maintain a proper balance between the loving God and the Holy God. Yes, God is loving, God is forgiving, but God is holy. He asks us to be holy because He is holy.

2 Corinthians 7:1 *Therefore, having these promises, beloved,*

let us cleanse ourselves from all filthiness of the flesh and spirit, perfecting holiness in the fear of God.

Let us notice that what Paul is saying in this verse is a commandment; *let us cleanse ourselves from all filthiness of the flesh and spirit, perfecting holiness in the fear of God.* You may say that God, through Jesus Christ, has cleansed us - that the blood of Jesus has already cleansed us.

While this is true, what then is the purpose of Paul commanding us to be cleansed? Through the cleansing received by faith, we also need to work out our cleansing from filthy things. As we have been cleansed by Jesus Christ, we need to live in that cleansing power day after day. How can we really walk in the power of cleansing day after day? Simply put, we will be able to cleanse ourselves when we realize that we are dirty. In other words, we have to see ourselves as being dirty day after day. We have to be very sensitive to the dirt of the world coming into us as we walk in our daily lives.

Unfortunately, we often live our spiritual lives filled with vain words. We are all familiar with the prayer, "Lord please cleanse us of our sins," but prayed without real remorse or conviction. To this the Lord will say, "do you see any filthiness in your life?" We will then reply, "We don't know, but do the work, because that is Your job. Try to find the filthiness in us and cleanse us!" However, God does not work this way. When we truly feel the dirt, we will feel convinced, broken hearted, hating ourselves, and like a little child coming to his mother saying, "oh please cleanse me!" When we can see the dirt, we will not be able to bear our state.

If we are living in the Spirit, we would not be able to bear dirt coming into us. When the dirt comes to us we will be able to feel that we are dying, choking, unable to breathe, and then we will cry out, "Lord have mercy on me, rescue me, cleanse me!" God honors such a prayer, because it is a true prayer coming from a crying heart. God then sends his cleansing Spirit and restores us to a holy life. In this way, we can live daily as a holy people, related to the holy God.

> 1 Peter 1:16 *because it is written, "Be holy, for I am holy."*

> Hebrews 12:14 *Pursue peace with all people, and holiness, without which no one will see the Lord.*

This is a serious statement! Without holiness, no one will see the Lord. We need to acquire a serious life.

Philippians 2:12-13 *¹² Therefore, my beloved, as you have always obeyed, not as in my presence only, but now much more in my absence, work out your own salvation with fear and trembling; ¹³ for it is God who works in you both to will and to do for His good pleasure.*

We may understand the phrase, *work out our salvation*, but we must really take heed of the other phrase, *with fear and trembling*. Let us think for a moment about these words. Paul tells us to work out salvation with fear and trembling because he knew that there are many things hindering us from working out our salvation. We find ourselves thinking, "Yes we are saved, and that is all." Peter describes this type of person as a shortsighted person (2 Peter 1:9). We must work out our salvation with fear and trembling.

Ephesians 5:14 *Therefore He says: "Awake, you who sleep, arise from the dead, and Christ will give you light."*

Jude 1:24 *Now to Him who is able to keep you from stumbling, and to present you faultless before the presence of His glory with exceeding joy.*

We need to understand that sometimes our motives are very self-centered. When we are self-centered, combined with the evil world around us, we lose our sense of the Holy God, and we lose our own holiness and our call to be a holy people. This grieves God, and leaves us powerless.

Restoring the original spring of Pentecost

Let us remember that we are still speaking about how to receive a new infilling of the Holy Spirit, an infilling which is related to our goal; ministering to the generation. This is an infilling that actually brings to us a new anointing of Elijah and John the Baptist.

The second principle is: restoring the original spring of the day of Pentecost. What does this mean? This is actually a very important issue but one that people rarely talk about. I would like to share a secret from my own life. When God revealed this principle to me some years ago, I could not find the daring to share it with others. I knew that it would be completely unfamiliar to people and so I kept it to myself for years. In due time, the Lord released this truth to be shared and it was well understood.

Since the fall of Adam, the Holy Spirit was cut off from man. Hence, evil increased because the Holy Spirit is the

One who keeps man in holiness.

> Genesis 6:3 *And the Lord said, "My Spirit shall not strive with man forever, for he is indeed flesh; yet his days shall be one hundred and twenty years.*

The Holy Spirit departed from man. If we are sensitive enough, and rooted in the Bible, we will discover the person of the Holy Spirit to be very gentle, very kind, very sensitive, and very loving to mankind. He loves to dwell inside man; this is His preferred home and dwelling place.

However, after the fall and the flood, it seemed like His dwelling place was lost. He continued to watch over man, from generation to generation, watching to see if there was anyone who would allow Him to come and dwell in him. However, no one was ready. He continued to watch with grief, desiring a dwelling place. Although He is living in the throne of the heavens, his favorite dwelling place is within the heart of the contrite and humble.

> Isaiah 57:15 *For thus says the High and Lofty One who inhabits eternity, whose name is Holy: "I dwell in the high and holy place, with him who has a contrite and humble spirit, to revive the spirit of the humble, and to revive the heart of the contrite ones.*

It is clear from this verse that God has two favored places; His highest place and in the heart of the contrite. The Holy Spirit was very grieved because He lost one of His favorite places to dwell in. Because He could not find a place on earth among men, He continued to watch over people throughout the generations.

One day He was so pleased because he finally found the man! He now knew that He could come to earth again and dwell in the heart of man. Because he was so excited, he could not come slowly. He acquired the picture of a dove with wings, to fly quickly to the Jordan River, and into the man of Jesus Christ to dwell within Him. He had restored His place on earth again in the heart of a man; Jesus incarnate. After waiting for some time, He knew that He could find a place in every heart of the believer and follower of Jesus. When Jesus finished his work on the cross, ascended, and poured the Spirit of God, He was able to restore again His dwelling place in the heart of man. However, there is another mystery.

When He filled the heart of man, He began to flow from the heart of man, like a river, to another place. Where is this place? It is where the believers gather; the Church of God.

> John 7:38 *He who believes in Me, as the Scripture has said, out of his heart will flow rivers of living water.*

He began to flow from the heart of men and formed a river. We can now see that there are two main sources of the Holy Spirit which a person can receive the infilling from. We can receive the filling from the throne of God because after the day of Pentecost the closed heaven was opened and the Holy Spirit was poured out. Jesus ascended and opened the heavens, which had been closed since the fall of Adam. Since the day of Pentecost, we can now receive the repeated infilling from the throne of God through an open heaven. We can also receive the infilling of the Spirit, from the river in the Church of God.

Why did God give the Church such an economy - to be able to always have the river of the Holy Spirit within the Church when we can receive the outpouring from the heavens? There must be a reason behind this. It is because God knows that there is a time when the Church sleeps.

Do you remember the parable of the 10 virgins who all fell asleep at midnight? It refers to the Church of God that sometimes falls asleep. Actually, history tells us that during the Middle Ages the Church of God was sleeping. This happens because when believers sin and do not repent, their sins can gather and form a cloud in the heavens. This can again block the opening of heaven and prevent the pouring of the Holy Spirit from above.

During a difficult time when the Church is sleeping, there are those who still hunger for the Holy Spirit. It is during this time that those who yearn for the infilling will mysteriously receive the Holy Spirit, through the river in the Church of God, without realizing they received this filling from the river. They do not see the river but they come to the Lord according to His word in the Bible. They prepare themselves by asking God to come and fill them without realizing that the clouds now block the heavens. However, because God is faithful, the Holy Spirit will come from the river flowing through the Church and fill these people.

It is dangerous for believers to continue sinning without serious repentance, because this again closes the heavens that were opened on the day of Pentecost. The heavens were opened with an immeasurable price, and the cost was the death of the Son of God. And because of our laxity we do not take sin seriously and thus bring clouds to block the open heavens again.

> Isaiah 44:22 *I have blotted out, like a thick cloud, your transgressions, and like a cloud, your sins. Return to me, for I have redeemed you.*

It is clear from this passage that sin can cause clouds, and this can block the heavens. The prophet Isaiah knew that the heavens were closed because of this cloud. His cry and prayer was, *Oh that you would rend the heavens and come down, that the mountains might quake at your presence.*

My dear friends, I tell you the truth. Sadly, believers are now receiving the infilling of the Spirit from the river in the Church, while the richest source of the Pentecost is no longer available. There are a lot of clouds now blocking our open heaven. Of course, the heavens cannot be closed again in the way it had been in the past; it is open still. Nevertheless, these clouds cover the opening and prevent the original pouring of the day of Pentecost. What a loss this is, for the outpouring from heaven is very pure, rich, and full of power. When this comes to our hearts and flows out of our hearts, it is still a river, and still living water, but not as rich as the pouring that directly comes from above.

However, when the day comes and the Church of God is awakened to restore their whole inheritance, and completely deal with the clouds, we can again receive the full outpouring of the day of Pentecost. Then the five main offices of the Spirit will also be released again in their fullness. The five offices are mentioned in Ephesians 4: apostles, prophets, teachers, pastors, and evangelists. When these offices are released in their fullness, there will be no more division within the Church of God. Different sectors of the Church will come together, because these offices will bring real and new revelation about Christ. Instead of each sector looking from their own angle to see only a part of the mystery of the person of Christ, they will receive the full revelation of Christ and agree on every theological point. We will become one body again.

There are many organizations, many missions that speak of oneness and love. They speak about allowing our beliefs to be different in our minds and hearts, but calling us to come together in love. This is not the biblical revelation that is written in Ephesians chapter 4. We must not only come together in love, but we must also come together in oneness of faith.

> Ephesians 4:13 *til we all come to the unity of the faith and of the knowledge of the Son of God, to a perfect man, to the measure of the stature of the fullness of Christ.*

This unity will occur when the fullness of the offices is released, and this requires the restoration of the original day of Pentecost.

However, there is an important principle here we must

remember. Despite this picture in the road of the Church of God at large, each person must fight their own battle, and pierce his own window through the clouds and acquire their own open window, connected to the original day of Pentecost. And this window will be with him wherever he goes. This is not a physical window, but a spiritual one. Through this window, he can receive the outpouring of the original day of Pentecost. This will completely change our hearts and our way of thinking, and can bring us into a position of real responsibility and real building for our generation. Be mindful, this is not something we can do for ourselves; only the Spirit of God can bring this burden, and with this burden comes the empowering to minister to this generation.

Responsibility toward the generation

Apostle Paul entreats his beloved disciple Timothy and speaks of the end times in 2 Timothy 2:2, *And the things that you heard from me among many witnesses, commit these to faithful men who will be able to teach others also.*

These words highlight the fact that apostle Paul desired the spiritual deposits to be kept and preserved for up to four generations. In this verse, the four generations are Paul, from Paul to Timothy, from Timothy to the faithful men, and finally, the faithful men to the others who were taught by them. Why did Paul have this preoccupation with the generations? It was because he understood the value of the spiritual deposits. He was given many revelations, and he knew that these revelations would keep the Church of God safe from divisions. If these revelations disappeared from the Church for one reason or another, divisions and problems would begin to appear in the Church.

> Acts 20:29-30 ^{29} *For I know this, that after my departure savage wolves will come in among you, not sparing the flock.* ^{30} *Also from among yourselves men will rise up, speaking perverse things, to draw away the disciples after themselves.*

From the first century, during Paul's own life, he could see in the spirit, the wolves that would come and do harm to the flock and speak perverse things. He understood that the only way to keep the Church safe was to keep the spiritual treasures and revelations safe. He knew that his life was coming to an end, so he turned to his faithful disciple Timothy. Entreating him to take care of these words, and all the revelations that he had heard from Paul, and to live them out; not only living out the truths for himself, but also passing them on to the faithful, those who knew that they were receiving treasures and those who would take on the responsibility for these treasures. And in turn, the faithful would pass it along to others, so that as long as the treasures were passed on, the Church would be safe.

It is interesting that Paul was thinking of four generations. During that time, a generation implied a century. This means that Paul was thinking ahead to four centuries in order keep the Church safe from divisions. If you study the history of the Church, it is amazing to find that the Church was actually kept safe from discord and united up until the 4th century. Divisions occurred after that, because the treasures and revelations began to be mingled with the world and its philosophies. The purity of the Spirit was no longer there.

In this very moment, you are receiving treasures. They are not my treasures, they are treasures that I received from the Lord and I am passing them on to you. Therefore, we must be treasure keepers, and must pass it on to those who are faithful. If you are willing to do this, you will then be entrusted by God, and will be anointed to minister to this generation. This is our responsibility - to be "treasure keepers." May God enable us to be truly faithful and pass it along to other faithful people.

V

UNDERSTANDING THE COVENANT RELATIONSHIP

The covenant relationship is the foundation for anyone who really desires to live in the fullness of the will of God. Unfortunately, very few have heard of teachings about the covenant.

Usually, we begin our spiritual life learning how to pray, reading the Bible, learning how to witness, and how to serve, which are all wonderful, but very basic. However, when one grows in the spirit, the Holy Spirit begins to open one's mind about the covenant relationship between God and man. If we are able to understand this important relationship in a deep and real way, and depend and work on it, then great changes will happen in our lives and ministry. What is a covenant relationship?

A simple example would be when two people come together to form a company. They will agree on some commitments, and each person will be committed to the other person. Usually, they are friends, and their friendship will grow closer because of their agreement for the company. If one of these people gets into trouble, he can call his partner and he will soon come to help because these two people are united under one purpose; the company. The same relationship is found in the covenant between God and man. When I am in trouble, I can call upon my Partner saying, "You are part of our covenant, so please come and help me!" He cannot refuse or ignore my cry and request. He has to respond because He is in a covenant relationship with me.

But if I do not correctly understand my covenant relationship God, then sometimes, I might say, "Lord heal me, you created me, you redeemed me, and I am your son," but deep within my conscience I know that although the son can call on his father for help, the father sometimes denies the request because the request is not suitable. However, the situation is different with partners of a company because they are in an agreement together. It is the same with the covenant relationship with God. We need to understand and grow in this truth.

Many years ago I came to understand the fullness of the

covenant relationship while searching God's words in the Bible. I thought I had already understood the covenant relationship. However, this new understanding of the relationship was so different and so much deeper than my past experiences. This shows that the Holy Spirit is eager to open our minds to this important relationship, day after day, and phase after phase. The more we understand and grow in this covenant relationship, our intimacy with God will be so different, our Christian impact on the world will be different, and our spiritual authority within the ministry will be different.

This is because when we are in a covenant relationship with God, it means that God will accompany us as a partner and companion. Wherever we go, He must go with us. Whatever we do, He must share in what we do. Do you know what makes Jesus so different in His life and His ministry? He was in a very close relationship with His Father.

> John 5:19 *Then Jesus answered and said to them, "Most assuredly, I say to you, the Son can do nothing of Himself, but what He sees the Father do; for whatever He does, the Son also does in like manner."*

Jesus sought daily to know what the Father was thinking

of, what the Father was doing, and accordingly did what the Father wanted Him to do. And in this way, Jesus and the Father were working together all of His days on earth, because there was a covenant relationship between Jesus and the Father. The biblical reference to this is in Isaiah 49, a chapter that speaks of the messianic prophecies about Jesus.

> Isaiah 49:8-9 *⁸ Thus says the Lord: "In an acceptable time I have heard You, and in the day of salvation I have helped You; I will preserve You and give You as a covenant to the people, To restore the earth, To cause them to inherit the desolate heritages; ⁹ That You may say to the prisoners, 'Go forth,' To those who are in darkness, 'Show yourselves.' "They shall feed along the roads, and their pastures shall be on all desolate heights."*

> Isaiah 49:6 *Indeed He says, 'It is too small a thing that You should be My Servant to raise up the tribes of Jacob, and to restore the preserved ones of Israel; I will also give You as a light to the Gentiles, That You should be My salvation to the ends of the earth.'*

The book of Isaiah speaks about Jesus being God's servant. And these verses are clear references about Jesus as the incarnate Christ. When Jesus was incarnated, he humbled himself to take the form of a servant. In verse 6 Isaiah speaks of a servant who will serve Israel, serve the gentiles, and be the light of the whole world. This is clearly a reference to Jesus. In verse 8, Isaiah speaks of the covenant between this servant and God. Therefore, we can see that Jesus was in a covenant relationship with God.

> John 8:29 *And He who sent Me is with Me. The Father has not left Me alone, for I always do those things that please Him.*

The Father was always with Jesus, because of that covenant relationship. When we understand this relationship and trust and work on it, then we will have the Lord as a constant companion in whatever we do, say, and wherever we walk. The covenant relationship is very fundamental and because of this, we need to look to Scripture to understand what it really means and how we can receive the light and the grace of it.

The Bible is composed of two different parts, the Old Testament and the New Testament. The word *testament* means covenant. In order to understand the word covenant, it is necessary to look in the Bible from the very beginning.

The first time we see this word in the Bible is in the story of Noah, just after he came out of the ark.

> Genesis 9:9 *And as for Me, behold, I establish My covenant with you and with your descendants after you.*

Later a covenant was established between God and Abraham in Genesis 15 and 17.

Before we continue, let us consider the fact that we are unable to find a covenant agreement mentioned between God and Adam. This was probably because Adam's relationship with God was a direct one and the closeness of the relationship was already there. It could be spontaneous and nothing hindered it. However, after Adam's fall, two main hindrances to this relationship occurred. There was an internal hindrance of sin, and an external hindrance from the enemy. Thus, separation and brokenness came into the relationship. Therefore, a certain form that would secure this relationship became necessary to restore it again.

God, in His love and mercy, knew that Adam now had a weakness inside him; his fallen nature that sometimes made him fear God and pull away from Him. The Bible tells us that Adam actually hid from God. In the meantime, God knew that the enemy was around Adam all the time and he had already planned to interfere with this relationship.

Sometimes the enemy comes and whispers, "Do you think that God can love you when you are a sinner, and you do not do anything good?" Other times the enemy comes and builds up a cloud, and we feel ourselves separated from God, as if He was far away and unreachable, and we are unable to sense His nearness. Because of this, God created the idea of a covenant relationship between man and God.

In this way, man could come into deep unity with the Father again. The Bible tells us that, before the fall, the relationship was already intimate and had the unity of a husband and wife. Afterwards, sin entered and broke this intimacy, which could not be restored because the fallen nature had distorted it. Even when God comes near, we cannot find the corresponding ability to build a relationship with Him because it has been distorted. Therefore, God created the idea of the covenant to re-secure and restore the distorted relationship.

However, after the fall, darkness came over the mind of man and it took some time for him to open his mind and be able to understand the covenant. Therefore, God's relationship with humanity was now moving gradually, step by step. God was observing and evil was spreading. God knew that if He explained the covenant to Adam's descendants, they would not be able to understand. Therefore, it seemed that God postponed the idea of the covenant until He washed the land with the flood. Humanity was corrupt with evil during the days of Noah. And the flood came to wash the land and destroy the corrupt creation. When Noah came out of the ark, He began to speak to him telling him that they would now enter into a covenant relationship.

It is helpful to create the atmosphere of the story when we read the Bible. The verses become vivid and filled with life, and then the Holy Spirit can open many secrets in the word of God. The idea of a flood was beyond anyone's understanding and was unimaginable. When Noah spoke to his generation about the flood, nobody could believe him. For a hundred years, not only was Noah building up the ark, but he was also preaching the message of the coming flood to his generation. Could you imagine preaching the same message for a hundred years? Sadly, no one else other than Noah's family was able to enter the ark.

We can also imagine that Noah's family members probably followed him into the ark because Noah was the head of the family and they had to obey him. Noah's family entered the ark, not out of full belief and trust, but out of familial duty and obligation. Maybe they expected nothing to happen and were speaking to each other saying, "We will probably spend the night in the ark with our father tonight but go back to our homes tomorrow."

However, Noah's family soon witnessed the enormity of the judgment, and the flood was dreadful. The Bible describes the flood in Genesis 7:11, *all the fountains of the great deep were broken up, and the windows of heaven were opened*, and in Genesis 7:23, *so He destroyed all living things which were on the face of the ground: both man and cattle, creeping thing and bird of the air. They were destroyed from the earth.* Where do these words come from? These words are from the impressions of the family members of Noah, who were observing everything from the ark.

The rain began, maybe lightly at first, but increased and increased, everyone began to fear and tremble because Noah's warning was coming true. For the first time, man, represented in that family, began to understand that judgment was real. And this scene was a warning of how dreadful the judgment could be. When Noah's family came out of the ark, everyone was trembling, and maybe reminded each other by saying, "Take care my brother, take care my wife, because if God becomes angry again for any reason, we will die in the flood. We saw with our own eyes, the limitless amount of water up there in His hands!"

Personally, this story shows me how merciful, gentle and kind God is. He knew what was going through the minds of the members of Noah's family. God does not like to build a relationship with trembling and fearful people. He desires to build love relationships as a Father. Man's fears are so deeply rooted in the fallen nature, and each one of us has deep rooted fears hidden within. Even if we are believers with a growing faith, it takes time to uproot the human fears and usually on different levels and different grades.

When Noah and his family came out of the ark, God began to sooth them and comfort them. Moreover, He was very clear when he said that there would never be a flood of that scale again. He is God, but when He has to judge man, he must resort to other ways. He understood that the flood was now a fearful thing to the human nature, and God did not want to create a fearful relationship. Because of this, the word *covenant* is mentioned for the first time after Noah stepped out of the ark. God said to them, "There will never be a flood again, and we will be closely knitted together in a covenant relationship." Through this, God established the first covenant with man.

> Genesis 9:9-17 *⁹ And as for Me, behold, I establish My covenant with you and with your descendants after you, ¹⁰*

and with every living creature that is with you: the birds, the cattle, and every beast of the earth with you, of all that go out of the ark, every beast of the earth. ¹¹ Thus I establish My covenant with you: Never again shall all flesh be cut off by the waters of the flood; never again shall there be a flood to destroy the earth. ¹² And God said: "This is the sign of the covenant which I make between Me and you, and every living creature that is with you, for perpetual generations: ¹³ I set My rainbow in the cloud, and it shall be for the sign of the covenant between Me and the earth. ¹⁴ It shall be, when I bring a cloud over the earth, that the rainbow shall be seen in the cloud; ¹⁵ and I will remember My covenant which is between Me and you and every living creature of all flesh; the waters shall never again become a flood to destroy all flesh. ¹⁶ The rainbow shall be in the cloud, and I will look on it to remember the everlasting covenant between God and every living creature of all flesh that is on the earth." ¹⁷ And God said to Noah, "This is the sign of the covenant which I have established between Me and all flesh that is on the earth.

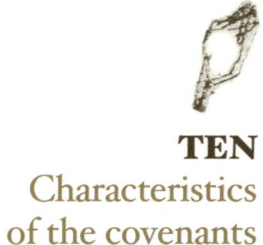

TEN
Characteristics of the covenants

In every covenant, there are certain characteristics. We need to understand the characteristics for each covenant in the Bible.

Characteristics of the covenant between God and Noah

The divine idea of establishing the covenant became the means of securing the relationship with man after the flood. God gave to Noah the condition that there would never be a flood again. Yet in this particular covenant, He did not require any conditions from Noah. Moreover, God gave a sign for this covenant with a rainbow. At this point, we have completed one phase in the history of God's covenant relationship with man.

We read in Genesis 10 that Noah's descendants began to multiply and fill the earth. Nevertheless, evil started to reappear. It is enough to read about Nimrod, the descendant of Ham, in Genesis 10:9, who was described as *a mighty hunter before the Lord*. In the original Hebrew language, the word *before* the Lord actually means *against* the Lord. The flood cleansed everything and Noah's family came out of the flood like holy men and women, but their descendants began to increase and with this, evil also began to rise up.

In Genesis 11 we read about the tower of Babel. The human plans for that tower was also against God. They were afraid of another flood, and they attempted to find a solution that would protect them from the flood. This meant that they did not believe or trust the covenant that God had made with Noah.

In the original Hebrew text, the bricks that they used in the building of the tower were of a material used to withstand water, which meant that they were still thinking about the possibility of a flood. If the rain began, they would go to the tower and close the door to keep safe. This meant that they did not believe God; even though God had told them there would be no more flood. These people were the descendants of Noah who knew of God's promise to never judge with a flood, and they also knew about the covenant. The descendants regarded this as a mere story and believed that the water could be poured from above again. So, in order to secure their own safety they began to build a waterproof tower.

God was grieved in His heart because they did not trust in Him anymore and were not interested in the covenant relationship that was based on love and comfort. Therefore, God confused their tongues and their project was nullified. Despite man's opposition and resistance, God adhered to His covenant and He did not destroy the earth as He had promised.

Let us again try to create the atmosphere of the stories of the Bible. It was clear that God was unable to find a person among the new family members of Noah, who could be close to Him. When Noah came out of the ark and the covenant was made, he was so close to God; as close as Adam had been in the garden. God actually used the same promises of blessings that He made with Adam, again with Noah. However, Noah died. Noah had three sons, but one of them was not close to God. Their descendants and the following generations also grew farther and farther away from God and did not care about their relationship with God. This grieved the loving God. God again searched for a person to restore the covenant relationship. After a while, God finally found him. It was Abraham.

Characteristics of the covenant between God and Abraham

> Isaiah 51:2 *Look to Abraham your father, and to Sarah who bore you; for I called him alone, and blessed him and increased him.*

God found Abraham and we see that He established a friendship with him; *and he was called the friend of God* (James 2:23). God began to establish another covenant with Abraham. This was proof that the first covenant with Noah was no more, because the descendants of Noah were no longer interested in a covenant relationship with God. If the covenant with Noah was still working with his descendants, there would be no need to establish another covenant with Abraham. Like any covenant, there must be an agreement between two parties. So God called Abraham near to Him and began to establish a new covenant.

God made two covenants with Abraham, one was mentioned in Genesis 15, and the other in Genesis 17. The first covenant was made as a result of a crisis in faith that Abraham went through.

> Genesis 15:2 *But Abram said, "Lord God, what will You give me, seeing I go childless, and the heir of my house is Eliezer of Damascus?*

Despite God's promise to Abraham to bless him with descendants, Abraham began to doubt. Thus, God arranged a covenant. So again, we see that God established a covenant to secure the relationship with man. When inner doubts started to grow inside of Abraham, it became a barrier in their relationship. God knew that there still remained some time before the birth of Isaac, and He was well aware of the doubts that Abraham would face in the years to come, which would break the relationship between Him and his friend Abraham. So, God began to establish a covenant, which was different from the one He had made with Noah.

God made a covenant with Noah without any apparent offerings or conditions from him. With Abraham however, God asked him to offer sacrifices cut into two halves and then for Abraham to wait for Him. In fact this was exactly the same manner that people of the surrounding tribes used in the days of Abraham. When people made covenants with each other, they would bring sacrifices, cut them in two and walk between the two halves. Walking between the two halves was a sign of the agreement between them. In those days, it was known that anyone who broke a covenant could be killed. God asked Abraham to do the same with Him. God used a relevant action that Abraham could easily understand. So Abraham brought animals and cut them into two halves and God passed through the two halves in the form of *a smoking oven and a burning torch*.

> Genesis 15:17 *And it came to pass, when the sun went down and it was dark, that behold, there appeared a smoking oven and a burning torch that passed between those pieces.*

God passed through as a fire but also as an illumination - a torch. This meant that God would illuminate the way of Abraham and his descendants whenever the darkness of the evil came upon them. However, this occurred at the end of a very long day for Abraham.

What was this day about? Again, let us try to create the atmosphere of the story. God knew that Abraham's main problem was a lack of faith and doubts. Abraham had no idea what the cause of his doubts was. Of course it was the big battle coming to Abraham from Satan. It was because

Satan began to see that this man would be a head of the believing host of God. So Satan tried to break Abraham's faith, knowing that once the head of the family was broken, the whole family would also lose faith. Satan came to Abraham saying, "You will never have a descendant, don't believe God, you are getting older, how can you have a son?"

Now it seemed that the time had come for the human being, represented in Abraham, to learn to fight against the enemy. Let us notice that this is the first occurrence in the Bible where God teaches man to fight the enemy. Abraham was under the attack of doubts, but he believed these doubts to be only thoughts, when in reality, they were the result of an evil power descending upon his mind. He could not see the evil spirits, and because of this, he could not fight them.

So, God planned something great. God asked him to offer the sacrifices and to wait for Him. Now, God and Abraham have already been in a friendship. When God asked Abraham to wait for Him, He knew that Abraham would wait because He knew that Abraham was a faithful person and a friend. Abraham gathered everything, prepared the animal sacrifices, and waited for God. I think that Abraham expected God to come soon, because usually God did not delay in coming to His friend. Abraham knew that when God comes He would deal with Abraham's problems.

So Abraham prayed, but God did not appear, and Abraham must have had many thoughts crossing his mind, "Where are You? Why are You late today? What happened? Maybe He is angry with me. I know that I have doubted and this does not please Him. But this is a fact that I cannot deny. I am too old to have a son. I apologize for making You sad, and so please come my Friend."

I would like to briefly pause here and share a story that touched my heart. It is a story of a young man who had recently graduated with a degree in engineering. This was about 20 years ago and during those days, engineering jobs in Egypt were very scarce. He was a gifted man who had a high-level degree in engineering, but was unable to find a job. In order to earn a living, he started a small business that was unrelated to his degree or studies.

There was a real man of God living in the same city. This man of God knew this young man and asked him, "Why don't you start an office related to engineering?" The young man replied, "There are no opportunities related to engineering these days. If I open up an engineering office there will be no clients." The man of God said, "My spiritual son, please prepare an engineering office for yourself, and God will bless you and let you work despite all the circumstances. But I have a request. You must bring your tithes to God." Then this man left, and the young man afterwards thought that there would be no tithes to offer because he was sure that he would not see an income generated from an engineering office. However, the young man went ahead and opened the engineering office. The man of God said to him, "Everything will work because *I know my Friend.*" He used the word *Friend*.

Soon a man came and sought the help of the engineer. He was a farmer from a village. At that time there was a law that required farmers to have a certificate from an engineer in order to use the irrigation machines. This farmer did not know anybody, so he left his village and went to a nearby city, and asked around for an engineer. The farmer was, at that moment, standing on the same street where the young man's office was located. And so the farmer was led to the office of the young engineer. The young man was amazed to see the farmer in his office. The farmer was served and the engineer received a good amount of money for his services. The young man took this money and went to the man of God and said, "Here is the money sent by your *Friend*."

Today, this engineer has a very blessed, large and expanded business, which began that day because of a man of God who knows his *Friend*, and can say on His behalf, authoritative words. You must trust me when I say this.

Even today, and until that day, God is searching for friends who can speak authoritative words on His behalf to bless the generation and to do what He wants. Everything begins from the friendship. We must establish a friendship with Him.

Now back to the story of Abraham. Abraham was waiting for his Friend. Abraham apologized and everything now seemed fine and so he asked God to come again. Then something happened that Abraham was not expecting at all. Instead, vultures came, attracted to the meat that was laid out. The meat could be spoiled because of these birds. This was not the first time for Abraham to offer sacrifices to God, because we know that he was always leaving with an altar and tent. He knew from past experience that after he offered the sacrifice and prayed, the fire of God would then come. But the sacrifice had to be intact. Abraham needed to wait for God's presence, the fire, so that he could enjoy his friendship.

However, there was no fire and the vultures were trying to eat the sacrifice. And if the birds got at the meat, the sacrifice would not be intact, and the fire would not come. Abraham was confused because this had never happened before, nevertheless, he began to fight and push the vultures away.

Genesis 15:11 *And when the vultures came down on the carcasses, Abram drove them away.*

What were these vultures? Herein lies the plan of God, to teach Abraham how to begin fighting with the enemy. He was not only teaching Abraham, he was teaching humanity how to fight the fight of faith.

1 Timothy 1:18 *This charge I commit to you, son Timothy, according to the prophecies previously made concerning you, that by them you may wage the good warfare.*

1 Timothy 6:12 *Fight the good fight of faith, lay hold on eternal life, to which you were also called and have confessed the good confession in the presence of many witnesses.*

This is inevitable. Nobody can be exempt from completing the fight of faith for his life. Everyone must fight the fight of faith if he really desires to walk with God. God knew that Abraham could not see the evil spirits, so He made a plan. He made Abraham offer the meat in the open air outside of his tent, to attract the vultures, and then God would hide, while Abraham would push and fight the vultures away.

The vultures were physically seen, but represented the

evil spirits coming into his mind as the source of doubts. Abraham fought the vultures for the whole day, until sunset. This means that it was a hard day for Abraham. Because God planned this, his fight was a fight against the evil spirits of doubt. Although God was hiding, He enabled Abraham to continue to fight until the end of the day. We are often faced with difficult days that are hard to get through from the start, but when we continue to fight, we find at the end of the day, a big release of blessings. Then we realize that it was the hindrance of the enemy from the start, trying to block the blessings. The enemy is cunning, and always desiring to destroy.

What happened to Abraham at the end of the day when sunset came? Abraham slept, because he was tired from the day and had no more physical energy. But let us not forget that this is a school of God for humanity, teaching us how to fight against the enemy. This means that during our fight with the enemy, we are expected to lose spiritual energy. Unfortunately, we are so short of breath during these fights, and we lose hope so quickly. We begin with enthusiasm and excitement, and as the day wears on, we soon start to feel discouraged, and eventually start to lose hope. I remember that I continued to pray for more than 20 years, waiting for God, for one thing. And God answered that prayer after 20 years. That long day of Abraham is not simply 12 hours, or even 24 hours, but it represents a long phase.

We must learn this principle of the Kingdom: when you are asking for great things, you must wait for a long time. If you want quick answers, you will have the small simple things of children only. Men and women of God, we must learn to fight the fight of faith for a long day. We must not be short of breath, but continue to push away the vultures and evil spirits, while waiting for our faithful God. Our faithful God will come again, and when he comes, He will come with the torch to illuminate and enlighten us, and will enable us to understand the whole story of the fighting, the darkness and the problems.

Then, on that same day the Lord made a covenant with Abraham.

> Genesis 15:18 *On the same day the Lord made a covenant with Abram, saying: "To your descendants I have given this land, from the river of Egypt to the great river, the River Euphrates."*

This story has actually inspired me a great deal in my personal life. Whenever I have a problem, I continue to pray and wait on the Lord, but I also ask Him, "Lord I need to understand, but I am waiting for You to choose the time to open my eyes." In Proverbs 28:5 it says, *those who seek the Lord understand all.*

Because we are so short of breath during our fights, we are unable to overcome the vultures and evil spirits. When evil spirits come to us, they do not only bring thoughts of doubts and lies, they also bring darkness. This darkness makes us unable to understand the ways of God.

> Genesis 15:12 *Now when the sun was going down, a deep sleep fell upon Abram; and behold, horror and great darkness fell upon him.*

The enemy not only wants to block blessings, but he wants to keep us in the darkness. When you are in the darkness, you are under the enemy's influence because he is the source of darkness. However, when we receive light, we see God and we are able to understand His ways. When we understand the ways of God, we can overcome Satan. But when we are in darkness we will stumble with God and we will be losers, not winners.

So dear friends, fight not only to bring blessings, but also to defeat the darkness. When a problem arises or you find yourself holding onto a promise, be patient, and continue to fight. And we must also ask the Lord for our understanding, but only in His time. Those who seek God will understand everything.

Let us now look at the second covenant of Abraham in Genesis chapter 17. The time span between the first and second covenant of Abraham was 13 years. Abraham was 86 years old at the time of the first covenant. And at the second covenant, he was 99 years old. The purpose of the 13 years of waiting between the covenants was given to Abraham to grow in the new faith he had received after completing the battle with the vultures.

We know that the first covenant was because of Abraham's crisis of faith. He had many doubts, and now he had finished the battle. God came with the torch and spoke to him and made a covenant. This means that Abraham at that point received a new measure of faith against the doubts. He began to believe again in the possibility of having a son; in fact, he was expecting it now.

However, it is important to realize that every gift received from God comes as a seed. This seed needs to sprout in order to turn into something that is established. God gave Abraham such a seed of faith after finishing this battle, and left him for 13 years to continue walking in that new faith he had received.

The source of doubt would assuredly come again, but

now with this new faith, Abraham would be victorious because he has faith against these doubts. God left Abraham for 13 years to exercise his new muscles of faith, and for sure the vultures came again but now he could overcome the doubts and did not need to stay a long day of fighting. Now he could finish his battle in a few hours, and maybe later on he could finish it in one hour. This is also the picture of what happens in our spiritual lives.

The first opposition over a matter can take a long day, or days, or even weeks. However, if we continue to fight we will break the power of that attack, and receive a gift. This gift is the much-needed faith, but it is always received as a seed. We need to continue on that walk for the seed to be opened up. The attacks will come again but we can be victorious in a shorter amount of time. Instead of weeks, it will now just be days, and then days will become hours.

God gave Abraham time to exercise his new faith and grow in it. Then Abraham's faith grew and God came again to establish another covenant with him.

The difference between the two covenants is very interesting. The previous covenant was related to the land, while this new covenant was related to the descendants of Abraham.

Genesis 15:18 *On the same day the Lord made a covenant with Abram, saying: "To your descendants I have given this land, from the river of Egypt to the great river, the River Euphrates."*

Genesis 17:2 *And I will make My covenant between Me and you, and will multiply you exceedingly.*

The second is a greater covenant because descendants are more precious than land, and more than that, God promised that Abraham would be a father of nations. Abraham became a father of faith, which was a great blessing. Notice that Abraham's wife was also included in this covenant.

Genesis 17:15 *Then God said to Abraham, "As for Sarai your wife, you shall not call her name Sarai, but Sarah shall be her name."*

A certain commitment was required as a sign of the covenant. In Noah's case, the sign was the rainbow. In the case of Abraham, the sign of the covenant was the circumcision. This sign has a very important significance, which was completely revealed in its fullness later in the New Testament.

Along with the sign of the covenant, there was also a condition of the covenant. God said to Abraham, *Walk before Me and be blameless* (Genesis 17:1).

> Genesis 17:1-3 *¹ When Abram was ninety-nine years old, the Lord appeared to Abram and said to him, "I am Almighty God; walk before Me and be blameless. ² And I will make My covenant between Me and you, and will multiply you exceedingly." ³ Then Abram fell on his face, and God talked with him, saying:*

It is interesting to note that the word *God*, mentioned three times in this passage, uses two different words in the Hebrew language. The word *Elohim*, and *El Shaddai* are used. When God asked Abraham to walk before Him and be blameless, the word for God was *Elohim*, which means *God who strengthens*. This meant that God would ask Abraham to do something but He would strengthen him to do it. The word for God in verse 3, *God talked with him, Elohim* is used again. However, in verse 1, the word used for God is *El Shaddai*, which means irresistible and unchanging. This meant that the covenant was secure, and no one could change or spoil it.

We know that in every covenant there are some privileges and some responsibilities. The privileges for Abraham are in verses 2 and 6.

> Genesis 17:2 *And I will make My covenant between Me and you, and will multiply you exceedingly.*

> Genesis 17:6 *I will make you exceedingly fruitful; and I will make nations of you, and kings shall come from you.*

What were the responsibilities? Abraham's responsibility was that through him all the families of the earth should be blessed - this means that from the start, God was asking Abraham to be responsible for the generation. It was as if God was saying to Abraham, "I bless you but you have to bless those around you, and let my blessings extend through you to all the generations."

The characteristics of the covenant of the descendants of Abraham

The covenants are like steps that are connected, leading up to the New Testament, which is the new covenant. We are in a covenant, but we are unable to live in the fullness of the blessings of the covenant unless we understand all the steps and series. First, we looked at Noah's covenant, and then Abraham's covenant, and now we can look at the covenant of the descendants of Abraham.

The descendants of Abraham are the nation of Israel. Isaac, Jacob, and the 12 tribes comprise the nation of Israel. This covenant was made with Moses as a representative of the whole nation. This occurred on Mount Sinai, and all the people were gathered at the foot of the mountain. Moses was up in the mountain with God making the covenant, but all the people of Israel also heard the voice of God.

> Exodus 19:5-6 *⁵ Now therefore, if you will indeed obey My voice and keep My covenant, then you shall be a special treasure to Me above all people; for all the earth is Mine. ⁶ And you shall be to Me a kingdom of priests and a holy nation.' These are the words which you shall speak to the children of Israel.*

It is clear that this was a covenant with not only Moses, but also with the people of Israel. After making this covenant, God gave the Ten Commandments, in chapter 20, which were the conditions of the covenant. We have a tendency to look at the Old Testament and the commandments as the *law* with negative connotations, but we do not understand the full revelation about the law. God does not give something that is bad. In Romans 7:6, Paul says that the law is holy. The problem is not with the law, but with our fallen nature, which cannot follow the law.

Because God is love and His covenant is a covenant of love; His law is a control of love in order to establish and protect love. When the people of Israel kept the law, the love was present, the covenant was established, and they were protected and blessed. However, when they broke the commandments, the love was severed, the covenant stopped working, and they were humiliated by the surrounding nations. And we know that they were pushed out of the land and forced into exile.

What happened after Mount Sinai? Unfortunately, the people soon broke the commandments, and because of this, a full generation died in the wilderness. The covenant made on Mount Sinai, was made with the people of Israel, so even though a full generation died, a new generation of people grew up. And because God is faithful, honest, and unchanging, He renewed the same covenant with the new generation at the end of their time in the wilderness.

Deuteronomy 29:1 *These are the words of the covenant which the Lord commanded Moses to make with the children of Israel in the land of Moab, besides the covenant which He made with them in Horeb.*

There is one purpose for the series of covenants made throughout history. God loves humanity, and desires to keep a covenant relationship with them. The first was the covenant of Noah, which was broken and made again with Abraham. Abraham was blessed with descendants to form the nation of Israel, and the covenant was made again with Israel. Again, the covenant was broken and a generation died in the wilderness. It was renewed with the new generation and then they finally entered the land. They lived in the land for generations. However, they broke the covenant many times so God sent prophets to them. They repented and the covenant was reactivated.

They continued to break the covenant and each time the covenant stopped working. This repeatedly occurred until the time of Jeremiah. Jeremiah began to say something important and new: God proclaimed that the fathers of Israel were constantly breaking His covenant, so now He was planning to make a new covenant. However, at that time, it was just a plan and with whom He was going to make this new covenant with was not yet clear. It was just a prophetic word spoken by Jeremiah.

Jeremiah 31:31-34 *[31] Behold, the days are coming, says the*

Lord, when I will make a new covenant with the house of Israel and with the house of Judah - [32] not according to the covenant that I made with their fathers in the day that I took them by the hand to lead them out of the land of Egypt, My covenant which they broke, though I was a husband to them, says the Lord. [33] But this is the covenant that I will make with the house of Israel after those days, says the Lord: I will put My law in their minds, and write it on their hearts; and I will be their God, and they shall be My people. [34] No more shall every man teach his neighbor, and every man his brother, saying, 'Know the Lord,' for they all shall know Me, from the least of them to the greatest of them, says the Lord. For I will forgive their iniquity, and their sin I will remember no more.

ELEVEN
The new covenant

As we understand the series and steps of the covenant relationship, this passage in Jeremiah brings to us a lot of light. God, as a Father and a healer, knew that man was unable to keep any type of covenant and would always break it. Thus, God needed a solution to this problem. God made a new plan, a new idea, to make a covenant, not with the people of Israel, but to choose one Israelite. This Israelite would be a sure person who would never break the covenant.

But, God knew that there were no Israelites who would always be able to keep the covenant, because all the descendants of Adam were corrupt with the fallen nature. Corruption came with the fall; the will of man became corrupt and so man could not keep anything. Therefore, God sent His Son incarnate into Israel, coming in the flesh as a descendant of David. Jesus was considered to be an Israelite. Can you see God's plan here? God the Father was now going to make the covenant with this Israelite, whose name is Jesus. Jesus was a sure person, faithful, someone who would never break the covenant. God did not stop there; He had another step in His plan. He would incorporate us in Jesus, so that the covenant would also work in us. There was only one way this could happen: when Jesus is considered to be the head of the new creation.

Jesus as the head of the new creation is parallel to Adam, who is the head of the old creation. Because we have all inherited the corruption of Adam, and being an extension of him, we are incorporated into him; he is our head. When Adam sinned, the result of sin passed onto us, and his corruption came into us. Now, Jesus came as the head of a new creation, having grace and righteousness, and this grace and righteousness came into us. It is important to understand this biblical fact.

> Romans 5:12 *Therefore, just as through one man sin entered the world, and death through sin, and thus death spread to all men, because all sinned.*

Romans 5:15 *But the free gift is not like the offense. For if by the one man's offense many died, much more the grace of God and the gift by the grace of the one Man, Jesus Christ, abounded to many.*

Romans 5:19 *For as by one man's disobedience many were made sinners, so also by one Man's obedience many will be made righteous.*

It is clear from these verses that there are two heads; Adam of the old creation who brought corruption, and Jesus of the new creation who brought righteousness and light. Jesus could keep the covenant without breaking it, and so Jesus is the surety of the covenant for us.

Hebrews 7:22 *by so much more Jesus has become a surety of a better covenant.*

Our covenant is assured and cannot be broken because it is not made with us, but made with Jesus, and we are in Him. Whenever we are in Him the covenant is working.

Theologically speaking, we are always in Him. But practically speaking, sometimes it is as if we are moved out of Him. Can this happen? Or is this suggestion a heresy? Remember that the fallen nature is still in us, and the fallen nature belongs to Adam. But the new nature is also in us, and the new nature belongs to Jesus. When we walk in the Spirit, we are in the new nature, connected to Jesus, and the covenant is working. But when we walk in the flesh, we are in the old nature, connected to Adam again, and the covenant is not working.

The Holy Spirit has put us in Jesus on the day when we were saved. So that stage is finished and we are already there, but the rest depends on our walk, day after day. When we walk in the Spirit, we are in the new position, in Jesus, in the new nature, with a new head, with the covenant. But when we walk in the flesh, it is as if we have left our position as the new man, turned back to our old nature to be with Adam again, connected with the old head and without the covenant. Can you now see the importance of walking in the Spirit day after day?

Let us read Hebrews 8:6-12 to fully understand the surety of the covenant.

> Hebrews 8:6-12 *⁶But now He has obtained a more excellent ministry, inasmuch as He is also Mediator of a better covenant, which was established on better promises. ⁷For if that first covenant had been faultless, then no place would have been sought for a second. ⁸Because finding*

fault with them, He says: "Behold, the days are coming, says the Lord, when I will make a new covenant with the house of Israel and with the house of Judah - ⁹ not according to the covenant that I made with their fathers in the day when I took them by the hand to lead them out of the land of Egypt; because they did not continue in My covenant, and I disregarded them, says the Lord. ¹⁰ For this is the covenant that I will make with the house of Israel after those days, says the Lord: I will put My laws in their mind and write them on their hearts; and I will be their God, and they shall be My people. ¹¹ None of them shall teach his neighbor, and none his brother, saying, 'Know the Lord,' for all shall know Me, from the least of them to the greatest of them. ¹² For I will be merciful to their unrighteousness, and their sins and their lawless deeds I will remember no more."

The passage tells us that this is a better covenant with better promises. Moreover, it is very clear that establishing a covenant between God and man is an unchanging idea in God's mind. Another important point is that God's promise to Abraham remained as is and did not change, but it was fulfilled in Jesus Christ.

Acts 3:25-26 *²⁵ You are sons of the prophets, and of the*

covenant which God made with our fathers, saying to Abraham, 'And in your seed all the families of the earth shall be blessed.' [26] *To you first, God, having raised up His Servant Jesus, sent Him to bless you, in turning away every one of you from your iniquities.*

Galatians 3:14 *that the blessing of Abraham might come upon the Gentiles in Christ Jesus, that we might receive the promise of the Spirit through faith.*

It is clear from these verses that the same blessing of Abraham is still working, but through Jesus Christ. We still have the same words that were given to Abraham: *I will bless you and you will be a blessing to all the nations of the earth.* Let us ask ourselves, are we blessed? And if so, are we blessing the nations of the earth?

The word of God tells us that the blessing of Abraham came to us through Jesus Christ. Therefore, we must take this seriously. It is a covenant relationship and because of this, this word is given to everyone and it has its expectations. God has blessed every one of us as a believer in Jesus Christ, with the same blessing of Abraham. Now God expects from every one of us to bless the nations. It is not necessary to travel all over the world to bless the nations. We can still bless the nations in different ways. We can bless the nations by prayer, and many other ways according to revelations by the Holy Spirit.

However, the main question is, do we understand our responsibility of the covenant? We must remember that a covenant consists of two parties. He blesses us and the condition is for us to bless others. Yet we are usually preoccupied with asking God for blessings for ourselves. We continually ask Him to bless us and He blesses. But God is asking us, "Are you blessing others around you?"

Think of this as if we were forming a company with a friend, and we put in one million dollars each towards the company under the agreement that the losses are divided and the gains are divided, with everyone knowing what belongs to whom.

And then the next morning, you ask your partner if you could borrow $500. Your partner says this is not part of the agreement. Then you will say, "I promise to give it back to you," and your friend is kind so she lends you the money. After a week, you ask again for $100. Your partner will say, "But this will affect our company and our work internationally." Still, you persistently ask, and because you friend is kind and loving, she will give it to you. Next week, you ask for another $1,000, and she will say, "You will spoil the agreement and it will affect our international work!" You answer, "But please give," and the friend is so kind that she will again lend you the money. But one day this friend will ask you, "Have you forgotten about our company and the purpose for which we made it?"

Would any of you accept this picture, this situation with your partner? This situation will spoil the company, and because the company has international branches, everything will be spoiled.

Now God has a company, which is called the Kingdom of God. And this company is an international company that has branches and extensions all over the world. The Kingdom of God must extend its branches all over the nations. It depends on roots, which God gives to us and in turn, we extend it. We receive from Him, and give to the branches so that the Kingdom may extend. This is the way the Kingdom of God grows and extends.

The Kingdom extends according to the covenant, according to the same promise to Abraham, because the promise has not changed. It was hindered because of Israel but was reactivated through Jesus Christ. God did not change the words that were given to Abraham because it is the rule of His Kingdom: *I bless you, so you may bless others.*

If we are unwilling to bless others, we can be assured that the blessing of God will not come to us. You may question this message at this point; "Does this mean our blessing will stop if our blessing does not extend to the nations? But this cannot be true because I am already receiving blessings!" Recall that there are two different categories of blessing. There is the general blessing on the material level for the believer and the unbeliever alike, and even for the wicked. But these are the special treasures of the heavenly blessings that are released through Jesus Christ.

This is the cause, my dear friends, why we are so poor in understanding of the mysteries of the word of God. The word of God is closed, not open. The treasures are not revealed to us despite the fact that there are countless treasures in the word of God; they are the blessing of the heavenly level. The condition for them to be released is through the covenant.

When we are ready to bless others, we will be blessed with all the heavenly blessings through Jesus Christ. The provisions will be opened up, and we will receive special blessings and then be transformed into His likeness. Grace will shine through us, and we will go out and bless others. We will come back to Him hungering for more because we now feed on this, no longer a man of flesh, but a man of the Spirit. We will now ask God to feed our inner man, and He opens His treasures. We receive and give, and receive and give; this is the covenant of God.

TWELVE
Experience the fruits and blessings of the covenant

To help establish a clear understanding of the covenant and begin to experience the fruits and the blessings of an active covenant, we must remember three points:

Understanding the covenant

Understanding the covenant is the first important principle, so we must continue to review the series and steps of the covenant so that we understand our relationship with God.

Believing the covenant

Believing is not an intellectual activity but a heart activity. You may begin believing by intellectually accepting what I am saying, but you must learn how to make the intellectual belief move down to your heart to create an active faith.

Making the covenant constantly active

We have seen that the covenant can be cut and stopped. However, it is now dependent on Jesus Christ. So the covenant can never be cut again, but we can be cut off from it, and we may not be able to receive from it.

In order to make the covenant constantly active, we must fulfill the conditions and understand the secret of the sign (circumcision). The condition is to walk before God and be blameless. Throughout history man failed because of the fallen nature, but now we have the Holy Spirit and the Holy Spirit enables us to fulfill the law, so we do not have an excuse. If we are really serious to walk straight with God, we will surely find the enabling through the Holy Spirit.

> Romans 8:2-4 *² For the law of the Spirit of life in Christ Jesus has made me free from the law of sin and death. ³ For what the law could not do in that it was weak through the flesh, God did by sending His own Son in the likeness of sinful flesh, on account of sin: He condemned sin in the flesh, ⁴ that the righteous requirement of the law might be*

fulfilled in us who do not walk according to the flesh but according to the Spirit.

This passage tells us that the Holy Spirit enables us to keep the condition. We must learn to acquire spiritual disciplines, pray regularly, read the word regularly, and obey it by the power of the Holy Spirit. In this way, our covenant will always be active.

Finally, the covenant is connected with circumcision. The covenant must always be active through circumcision. What is circumcision? Paul explains circumcision in New Testament terms.

Colossians 2:11-12 *¹¹ In Him you were also circumcised with the circumcision made without hands, by putting off the body of the sins of the flesh, by the circumcision of Christ, ¹² buried with Him in baptism, in which you also were raised with Him through faith in the working of God, who raised Him from the dead.*

The circumcision is a baptism in the action of the death and resurrection. Circumcision is the cutting of the foreskin of the member of the body, and Paul tells us that it is cutting the foreskin of the old nature. The problem with our modern theology is that it tells us that because we have been baptized in Christ, everything has been is completed and we do not need to do anything else. We take everything for granted. But this is not right because the circumcision relates not only to the old nature, but also relates to the heart in particular. Let us look at the biblical reference for this.

> Romans 2:28-29 *²⁸ or he is not a Jew who is one outwardly, nor is circumcision that which is outward in the flesh; ²⁹ but he is a Jew who is one inwardly; and circumcision is that of the heart, in the Spirit, not in the letter; whose praise is not from men but from God.*

We read in Romans 2:28-29 that circumcision is a matter of the heart in the Spirit. We need to understand that some parts of the word of God need revelation because there is deep meaning in them and cannot be understood by the mind. What does it mean to circumcise our heart in the Spirit? We must understand this because it is a very important issue.

It is the key that can make the covenant work for us. We have now learned and understood that we are still in the covenant of Abraham, through Jesus Christ, but this covenant needs circumcision, and Paul says that this circumcision is of the heart and not the flesh. As we read the Bible this way, we can pause here and begin to pray, "Lord this needs revelation, open my eyes, open the special blessings and give me the treasure hidden in this verse." We need to always keep our hearts sensitive, circumcised, so this needs to be revealed. I would like to share with you what I have received many years ago.

The heart has a cover on it like a foreskin. When we come to Christ, it is torn and cut like the foreskin of the old days. It becomes a living and sensitive heart. But the important point is that this foreskin can be formed again on the heart, due to the combined activity of the fallen nature inside of us, the spirit of the world outside of us, and our weakness.

Many times, we are deceived and take things from the spirit of the world without discernment, and we are unaware that we have been affected by the defilement around us. And then when the Holy Spirit shows us our defilement, we become serious and we repent and our sins are covered and forgiven. However, we do not realize that the repetition of this process can form the foreskin of the heart again, and thus the circumcision of the heart in the Spirit is needed again.

This is done in two ways.

The first way is through acquiring spiritual tools like fasting, self-denying, humbling ourselves, and sacrificing things; all of which cut the heart. Despite the fact that we do not like to sacrifice, when we sacrifice we cut our hearts. We do not like fasting, but when we cut food, we are cutting the foreskin of our hearts. We do not like to commit to get up for daily early prayer, but when we commit ourselves; we cut the foreskin of the heart.

The second way is to humbly accept the chastening of God. Look to the Bible to see the history of the men of God. The great men of God who were so close to Him and were His friends were chastened by Him, so that their heart would always remain sensitive. For example, Abraham was taken out of his land, he was cut off from his land and his family, and his heart was wounded. Abraham may have thought, "Ah, I need to be among my people back home, but I am going to obey God. I feel wounded and my heart is bleeding." Through this chastening, Abraham's foreskin was being removed. God also allowed famine to occur during the time of Abraham. He went to Egypt where his wife was taken for some time, and they were barren for so many years. There were many trials of faith. God was chastening Abraham to keep his heart circumcised.

Jacob faced many difficulties with Laban, with his two wives, the death of Rachel, and losing his son Joseph; it was to keep his heart always circumcised.

Joseph was sold by his brothers, falsely accused by Potiphar's wife, and put in prison. What was the purpose of all these trials? It was to keep his heart circumcised. And because of this, God entrusted all these men with great things.

Moses fled to Midian and endured 40 years of training in the wilderness. David experienced much trouble from Saul, fled to the caves in the wilderness, and endured the trials from his son Absalom. There was a great deal of trouble, pain and suffering. How could God allow these things to happen to His beloved David? All of these things were done in chastening; to circumcise his heart. We need to accept this. Let us conclude with Hebrews 12.

Hebrews 12:4 *You have not yet resisted to bloodshed, striving against sin.*

We need to learn how to labor in spirit up to the point of bleeding.

Hebrews 12:9-10 *⁹Furthermore, we have had human fathers who corrected us, and we paid them respect. Shall we not much more readily be in subjection to the Father of spirits and live? ¹⁰ For they indeed for a few days chastened us as seemed best to them, but He for our profit, that we may be partakers of His holiness.*

God wants us to share in His holiness, but He has to chasten us as our Father.

Hebrews 12:14 *Pursue peace with all people, and holiness, without which no one will see the Lord.*

This is the way to live and be holy. This holiness is inevitable because without holiness no one can see God. This is the way to live as the people of the new covenant, to bless and be blessed!

Now let us say together, Amen.

Anchor Publishing & Media hopes to deliver the message from heaven and to lead all people of all nations and languages to righteousness.